*En...*

"With something as elemental as the alphabet, Kolleen expands our minds and hearts into our truest identity in Christ. Her 'God says' truth and personal stories make this a book that's hard to put down. This is not simply Kolleen's story; it is a fresh way to understand how Father God is writing our #beYOU stories as well—He is changing our identity to make us more like His Son."

—**Dawn Marie Wilson**, founder—Heart Choices Today
www.upgradewithdawn.com

"Kolleen's book, *#beYOU*, encouraged me to *activate* change in my life, *become* the identity God already sees in me, and *confess* biblical concepts to believe these truths of transformation. Kolleen takes something as simple as the ABCs to communicate principles relevant for life change and spiritual formation. I related to her personal stories and felt like she truly understood my struggles. The ABC Girl inspired this Grin Gal to hunker in to God's love and be in him all he has for me. BeYOUtiful."

—**Kathy Carlton Willis**, God's Grin Gal, national speaker and author, including *The Grin Gal's Guide to Joy*
www.kathycarltonwillis.com

"This book is filled with encouraging words, biblical truths, and practical action steps to walk out your faith one letter at a time. Whether you're a new or seasoned believer, *#beYOU* will guide you on how to minister to yourself and others with the simple act of encouragement and becoming the person God created you to be."

—**Jayme Hull**, award-winning author, speaker, and host of *Face-To-Face Mentoring Podcast*
www.jaymeleehull.com

# #beYOU

## Change Your *Identity* *One Letter* at a Time

### Kolleen Lucariello

 **kml**BOOKS

**Published by KML Books**
**ISBN: 978-1-7345578-0-0**

Cover and interior design by Michelle Rayburn (www.MissionandMedia.com)
Photo for cover composition by Buco Balkanessi on Unsplash.com
Back cover headshot by Mabyn Ludke Photography
Editors: Brandi Ginty (www.inkible.co) and Michelle Rayburn

Updated and substantially edited from the previously released version, *The ABCs of Who God Says I Am*.

✳ ✳ ✳

## Dedicated to:

My girls: Sarah, Caroline, Lindsey, and Emery
It would fill me with great joy to know you've
discovered and embraced your true identity in Christ.
#beYOU. I love each of you immensely.

# Contents

Acknowledgments - - - - - - - - - - - - - - - - - - - ix

Introduction - - - - - - - - - - - - - - - - - - - - - xiii

A Is for **Accepted** - - - - - - - - - - - - - - - - - - 1

B Is for **Beautiful** - - - - - - - - - - - - - - - - - - - 9

C Is for **Changed** - - - - - - - - - - - - - - - - - - 17

D Is for **Desired** - - - - - - - - - - - - - - - - - - 23

E Is for **Established** - - - - - - - - - - - - - - - - 31

F Is for **Forgiven** - - - - - - - - - - - - - - - - - - 39

G Is for **God's Child** - - - - - - - - - - - - - - - - 47

H Is for **Holy** - - - - - - - - - - - - - - - - - - - - 55

I Is for **Image** - - - - - - - - - - - - - - - - - - - - 63

J Is for **Justified** - - - - - - - - - - - - - - - - - - 71

K Is for **Known** - - - - - - - - - - - - - - - - - - - 79

L Is for **Loved** - - - - - - - - - - - - - - - - - - - 87

M Is for **Mind** - - - - - - - - - - - - - - - - - - - 95

N Is for **New** - - - - - - - - - - - - - - - - - - - 103

O Is for **Overcome** - - - - - - - - - - - - - - - - 111

P Is for **Purpose** - - - - - - - - - - - - - - - - - - - 119

Q Is for **Qualified** - - - - - - - - - - - - - - - - - - 127

R Is for **Righteous** - - - - - - - - - - - - - - - - - 135

S Is for **Secure** - - - - - - - - - - - - - - - - - - - 143

T Is for **Treasured** - - - - - - - - - - - - - - - - 151

U Is for **Understand** - - - - - - - - - - - - - - - - 161

V Is for **Victorious** - - - - - - - - - - - - - - - - 169

W Is for **Wise** - - - - - - - - - - - - - - - - - - - - 177

X Is for **eXcluded** - - - - - - - - - - - - - - - - - 185

Y Is for **Yoked** - - - - - - - - - - - - - - - - - - - 193

Z Is for **Zealous** - - - - - - - - - - - - - - - - - - 201

Afterword - - - - - - - - - - - - - - - - - - - - - - - - 209
Notes - - - - - - - - - - - - - - - - - - - - - - - - - - -211

# Acknowledgments

People come into our lives for seasons and reasons. Some seasons are short, while others stick around for a very long time. The Lord had a reason the day I met my friend's brother in the eighth grade and crushed on him throughout middle school. Our seasons together have been full of adventure and adversity, but we've always found a reason to stand in our commitment to one another. Pat is my greatest supporter who always encourages me to try, even when he knows I might need to fail. He is a man of grace and showers it upon me daily. Pat, you are the most faithful, loving, and patient man I know. I cherish the memories we've made together throughout the last thirty-seven years and look forward to making many more. Every day we share together, I love you more. Thank you for showing me such unconditional love and allowing me to always be me.

My beautiful children: Adam, Sarah, and Matt. You lived through the journey of change that the Lord took me on, *and* you survived. I weep when I realize you've seen me at my worst and yet you still call me a good mom. I adore you all and am blessed God allowed me to be the one who is your momma. Jeffrey, Caroline, and Lindsey, thank you for marrying into our family. We are delighted God included you on our pilgrimage through life. I pray that you all allow the Lord to establish your steps as well as take you on the journey to become the people He designed you to be.

Thank you, Caroline and Kenda Beckwith for using your gifts and talents to help me clean up the original draft of this manuscript and clearly write what the Lord was putting on my heart. Thank you, too, for showing me the value of a thesaurus.

My original Bible study girls: Christine Garrett, you've stuck with me during the laughter and the tears, the highs and the lows, the clarity and the confusion. You have spoken truth that has corrected me and encouraged me, but most importantly you have loved me—just as I am. When others walked out of my life, you remained a true and faithful friend. I am a better me because of you. I am honored to serve the body of Christ together with you as we Activ8Her for Him.

Cindy Shipley Blaske, I treasure the memories of our time in the Word together. Well done good and faithful servant. We miss you.

Sue Phillips and Kecia Schell, I had the vision for this book, and you were willing to walk through the very first pages of a rough draft with me. I have sweet memories of our Thursday nights together and the book that was birthed because of them. Thank you for your comments, insights, and suggestions. You ladies blessed me so much.

Jackie, Donnie always wanted to make a difference in people's lives. His death changed many people forever, me included. I'm sorry we lost him for the remainder of our time here, but I think he would be so pumped to know that my relationship with the Lord grew out of his graduation from here to there. I can't wait for the reunion.

Pastor Don and Diane Schell, you two have always been such an important part of my life and a huge foundation in my faith. Your family is so very special to me, and I am blessed that the Lord allowed me to build so many of my memories around each member of the Schell family. I love you all so much.

Dad and Mom, thank you for dragging me to church every Sunday and introducing me to Jesus. I am forever grateful for you. I love you both.

There have been several pastors whom, over the years, the Lord has had me sit under for teaching, training, rebuking, and correcting. Thank you for pouring the Word of God into me. Thank you, Kathy Carlton Willis and the WordGirls for sharpening my skills and convincing me I was a writer.

Thank you, Brandi Ginty for sowing seed into me and the ministry of Activ8Her. I appreciate your heart and how the Lord has gifted you to help others capture their words, compose their voice, and create their dreams to be Inkible.

Thank you, Michelle Rayburn for encouraging me to republish the ABC book and using your incredible gifts and talents to partner with me to make it happen. I am in awe of your ability to capture my personality and my heart from front cover to the back.

And thank you to everyone who read the *ABCs of Who God Says I Am*, or a blog, or an article and encouraged me to keep writing. My writing is proof that God may have plans for us that are different than our own.

Jesus, thank you for saving me. Thank you for allowing me to serve You. I adore You.

# Introduction

When I first wrote *The ABCs of Who God Says I Am*, I had no idea I was writing a book. I was simply wrestling with depression over what I perceived to be my lack of purpose. Clearly, I wasn't quite as ready for the empty nest as I thought I was. Struggling to find my place in this new season, the Lord opened the door for me to assist family friends who needed daycare. It was during this time that—as I read a children's book to one of my little friends—the Lord began speaking to my heart about my identity.

I began to see different words other than those rudimentary images that had been chosen for each letter in the book. *A* no longer stood for apple, and *B* wasn't about a ball. The words I began to see were words that I sensed the Lord was using to describe me. Well, not only me, but you too. He began to show me that He views us far differently than we view ourselves, and He took me on a journey. I am a pretty simple girl, and I enjoy when the Lord makes things easy for me to understand. I believe that is exactly why He had me go through the alphabet.

On this journey, I discovered so much about who we really are through the lens of the Word. I learned that we are **a**ccepted, no matter what we have done or where we've been. We are **b**eautiful to behold through the eyes of our Father. We have been **c**hanged—no longer the same as we once were. We are **d**esired by the God of the universe. We have been **e**stablished, **f**orgiven, and made **f**ree. We are **G**od's children, and because of that we are **h**oly—made in His **i**mage. We are **j**ustified from our sins. We are **k**nown and **l**oved. We have been given the mind of Christ and have been made new—able to overcome. God has given us a purpose. We are qualified by God to share in His inheritance. We are righteous and secure; nothing can separate us from Him. We are treasured, understood, and victorious—full of wisdom, excluded from the world, and yoked to the King of Kings and Lord of Lords. We are now able to live a zealous life in the joy of the Lord.

When the publisher for the first edition of this book closed its doors, I wasn't sure what to do with the book next. So, I did nothing! But, I suspected God would not allow its content to be discarded completely; identity is too important of a message for His people these days. I was right—and here we are again. Although some content is the same and some might be similar, a bit of it is new altogether—for example, the title. One thing remains the same: God desires that we walk in the fullness of who He created us to be.

As we walk through the twenty-six letters together, you'll find an opportunity at the end of each chapter—an exercise to Activate, Become, and Confess. It really is as simple as ABC. I encourage you to pause and reflect on the questions and next steps as you:

**A – Activate** and start the work of seeking God for what he wants to change in you.

**B – Become** by stepping into the identity God designed for you and learning how to #beYOU.

**C – Confess** by declaring in faith what God's Word says about you and committing to embrace who you really are in Christ.

Thank you for taking this journey with me as we allow God to change our identity one letter at a time. He made it quite clear to me, and I hope He makes it quite clear to you, that there are some things we are never too old to learn.

# A Is for *Accepted*

## God Says I Am ACCEPTED.

To the praise of the glory of His
grace, by which He made us
*accepted* in the Beloved.

—Ephesians 1:6, emphasis mine

**Accepted**: *To take or receive (something
offered); receive with approval or favor.*[1]

Thinking back to my teenage years still brings painful memories of how desperate I was to be accepted by others. Gaining the acceptance of my parents, my siblings, and my peers was so important to me that, many times, I would allow myself to do things I knew were wrong because this desire was so great. I was extremely insecure. I'm sure we could each share a story or two of the moments when we knew better but failed to act on that knowledge.

One of those instances for me was the day I allowed myself to be talked into hitching a ride on the fender of a friend's bicycle down a very long and steep hill. I didn't want to ride on the fender, but everyone else had a bike, and no one wanted to wait for me to make the walk. So, on the fender I sat—until we found ourselves at the bottom of the hill where my friend hit those dreaded small gravel stones that had just been put down by the highway department.

I don't actually recall much of the next few moments. What stands out for me still to this day, though, was my little body flying through the air and then my face hitting the ground and skidding across those stones on the pavement. A call to my parents, an emergency room visit, and stitches above my eye— all because I wanted to be received by friends with approval and favor.

What I have learned (most often the hard way) is this: The more I tried to win acceptance from others, the more I needed to compromise what I knew was right in order to get it. It took some time for me to realize that when we live for the acceptance of man, we risk becoming someone other than who the Creator has fashioned us to be. If you allow yourself to live for the acceptance of others for too long, you won't know who you are or what you really believe. Your life becomes a lie. A struggle begins to stir within your mind and soul, and deep inside you know that no matter how hard you want acceptance, you question whether you will really gain it from people.

That struggle between right and wrong can be an overwhelming battle at times. There is a voice inside you longing to speak, a message that needs to be heard, but fear of being "unacceptable" to others keeps you from sharing it. There are stands that need to be taken and challenges that should be made, but the fear of looking foolish can keep us from taking and making them.

Longing for acceptance is not a new thing. We shape ourselves around society and have allowed ourselves to be intimidated by the status quo. We, like those before us, have sought the approval of men rather than God.

> Nevertheless, many even of the rulers believed in Him, but because of the Pharisees they were not confessing Him, for fear that they would be put out of the synagogue; for they loved the approval of men rather than the approval of God. (John 12:42–43 NASB)

There were leaders who believed that Jesus was who He said He was, but because they loved the approval of man, they would not confess Him. They allowed the fear of other people to keep them from experiencing Jesus in all His fullness. It is a tragedy when fear prevents us from experiencing all that Jesus has for us.

What a tragedy it would have been if Mary had allowed the opinion of others to keep her from experiencing an intimate moment she shared with Jesus. Mary anointed Jesus's feet with expensive perfume, and although the disciples didn't accept it, Jesus did. In fact, He defended her:

> Then, six days before the Passover, Jesus came to Bethany, where Lazarus was who had been dead,

3

whom He had raised from the dead. There they made Him a supper; and Martha served, but Lazarus was one of those who sat at the table with Him. Then Mary took a pound of very costly oil of spikenard, anointed the feet of Jesus, and wiped His feet with her hair. And the house was filled with the fragrance of the oil. But one of His disciples, Judas Iscariot, Simon's son, who would betray Him, said, "Why was this fragrant oil not sold for three hundred denarii and given to the poor?" This he said, not that he cared for the poor, but because he was a thief, and had the money box; and he used to take what was put in it. But Jesus said, "Let her alone; she has kept this for the day of My burial. For the poor you have with you always, but Me you do not have always." (John 12:1-8)

The disciples couldn't understand the significance of this act, but Jesus did. He knew the spiritual implication behind it. Have you ever known something to be true in your heart, but would not allow yourself to speak it for fear of what others around you would think and say? When it comes to our faith, sometimes we experience an overwhelming sense of fear that we are going to look or sound foolish if we speak up for what we believe in. The truth is there is a good chance that you *will* be looked at foolishly. We can read that in 1 Corinthians 1:18: "For the message of the cross is foolishness to those who are perishing, but to us who are being saved it is the power of God" (NIV).

With today's view that everything and anything goes, a Christ-centered view is not widely and openly received, even among Christians. Speaking about what God is doing in your life or a revelation He has given you from His Word might not sit well, especially if it brings conviction to others. But the acceptance of our Savior must take precedence over being accepted by others.

For me, acceptance means to find a place where I can go and be my *true* self and know that I will be shown the grace, love, and mercy we all long for. I will never have to fear being cut off because I didn't adhere to the standards of society. This doesn't mean that everything I say or do is right and I should never be confronted. Acceptance means that no matter what mistakes I make or how mad I make others, they will still accept me for who I am and love me just the same. Sounds a little unconditional, doesn't it? Well, that is what Christ's acceptance brings.

Once I grasp the knowledge that my acceptance by God isn't based upon my performance, and I really believe it in my heart, I won't need to find my acceptance in other people. What would my life look like if I didn't work so hard for the acceptance of *people* and realized that no matter what, I am always going to be accepted by God? I might not feel the need to try to impress others with the clothes I wear, the car I drive, or the job I have. Maybe once I realize that God has forgiven so much in my life and accepted me, it would make it easier to live out Romans 15:7, which says, "Therefore, accept one another, just as Christ also accepted us to the glory of God" (NASB).

As a wife, mother, and friend, I still fight the battle of searching for my acceptance in who I am and who others see me as, rather than in *whose* I am. It is challenging to remember that no matter what is going on around me or how I feel, I am accepted by God. Others may reject me and find me completely unacceptable, but to the God of the universe, I was found worthy of acceptance. How completely incredible is that?

When I read the following passage from Ephesians, my heart swells:

> Blessed be the God and Father of our Lord Jesus
> Christ, who has blessed us with every spiritual

blessing in the heavenly places in Christ, just as He chose us in Him before the foundation of the world, that we should be holy and without blame before Him in love, having predestined us to adoption as sons by Jesus Christ to Himself, according to the good pleasure of His will, to the praise of the glory of His grace, by which He made us accepted in the Beloved. (Ephesians 1:1-6)

It is humbling for me to think that He has blessed me with every spiritual blessing and chose me before the foundation of the world. He also knew He would call me His own, and He provided a way for me to be accepted by Him.

God has accepted me.

Just as I am, He has accepted me. When I offered my heart to Him—just as the definition of accepted says—He received me with approval and favor.

From the original Greek, *charitoo* is translated as *accepted* and means "highly favored."[2] In a world where there is very little acceptance of one another, God wants us to know and understand that we are accepted by Him.

I am highly favored.

You are highly favored.

We can find the acceptance we have been longing for in Jesus Christ.

We will change our identity one letter at a time as we remember there is no need for us to jump on anyone else's fender; doing so only leads to crashes and scars. The God of the universe has accepted us as His own; what more could we ask for?

Activate, Become, and Confess as you seek to change your identity one letter at a time.

## Activate – Start the Work

- What do some people do for acceptance?
- Which of the things you listed have you tried? What were the results?
- What can you do right now to break free from seeking the acceptance of others?

## Become – Come into Existence and #beYOU

- Read Psalm 56. Can you think of a time when you experienced a situation where you could relate to the psalmist? Where did you put your trust then?
- What might have gone differently if you had fully trusted in God?
- How does this psalm inspire you for the next challenge you face?
- Describe how it feels to know that God is for you (vs. 9).
- What false beliefs can you relinquish as one *accepted* by Christ?

## Confess – Declare in Faith

I declare today that I will live my life for the acceptance of One. I will seek You, Father, whenever I am afraid. I will trust in You and You alone, Lord. I believe You are for me and not against me. I have been and always will be accepted by You, Lord. I will fear no human; what can anyone do to me when I have you for a Defender?

## *Let's pray:*

Oh Lord God, thank You for accepting me! Thank You for receiving me with gladness and approval. Father, help me to overcome the addiction I have to finding acceptance from others. Help me to release to You my desire to be liked by others and the longing I have to seek approval in others. You have accepted me, and I will no longer surrender to the lie that my approval rating is found in man. Thank You, Jesus, for settling this truth within my heart. In Your name I pray. Amen.

# B Is for *Beautiful*

God says I am BEAUTIFUL.

You are completely *beautiful*, my beloved!
You are flawless!

—Song of Solomon 4:7 LEB, emphasis mine

**Beauty:** *the quality present in a thing or person that gives intense pleasure or deep satisfaction to the mind, whether arising from sensory manifestations (as shape, color, sound, etc.); a meaningful design or pattern, or something else (as a personality in which high spiritual qualities are manifest).*[3]

A few years ago while watching television, I saw a commercial for Dove soap that showcased an ad campaign on beauty. The commercial featured several young girls who shared their definitions of beauty. Wondering about how to define beauty piqued my curiosity, so I began to search through the company's website. Here's what I discovered: Dove developed an advertising campaign about true beauty based on the opinions of a range of women. The goal was to spark a national discussion in order to widen the definition of beauty. The website included statistics that stated, "Only 4% of today's women describe themselves as beautiful (up from 2% in 2004)." The report also stated that 81% of US women held a strong belief that there has been an unrealistic standard of beauty set by the media and advertising industry, one that is unachievable by most women.[4]

The company has some heartfelt videos on learning to love yourself just as you are. It's a great message. However, the videos leave out a very important aspect of beauty. How will we ever stop obsessing over our flaws on the outside and begin to be comfortable with how we look if we leave out the spiritual aspect? I truly believe it is God, through His Word, who needs to teach and show us what real beauty is. Isn't it intriguing that one of the definitions of beauty at the beginning of this chapter is "a personality in which high spiritual qualities are manifest"?

When I was younger, my appearance was excruciatingly important to me. I wasted much time fussing and worrying over how I looked. One area of great insecurity for me was the split between my front teeth. When I looked in the mirror, all I saw was a very large gap, and let me tell you, it tormented me. Well, that and my brother who relentlessly picked on me about it, which made the gap seem wider than it really was.

I never felt comfortable smiling because I believed that when I did, all eyes focused on my teeth. I begged for braces, and when the dentist told me I didn't need them, I cried. "How could he say that? If he had a gap like this in his teeth, then he would understand." With his dental wisdom, he encouraged me to be patient, promising me that they would grow together eventually.

That didn't help me.

I wanted them fixed now. As in, *right now*. And if he wouldn't help me, well then, I would simply take matters into my own hands. I'm a pro at taking matters into my own hands.

The insecurity led me to begin subjecting my mouth to a variety of torture devices ranging from rubber bands to the metal backs of barrettes—anything I could wrap tightly around my two front teeth that I thought might help my teeth grow together was fair game. What a chuckle this gives me now, thinking of how silly I must have looked. I wanted to look good, yet I was willing to do things that made me look ridiculous! And while I sought beauty on the outside to make an impression on others with my looks, rarely did I give thought to how I looked on the inside.

Looking back, I must confess I was rather ugly most times— not because of my outward appearance so much (although there were times there was truth to that as well) but because when I opened my mouth, it wasn't my teeth that made me ugly; it was the ugliness people heard coming out of me.

We are sorely mistaken when we believe our beauty has everything to do with physical appearance. We miss God when this becomes our focus. Here's why: "Like a gold ring in a pig's snout is a beautiful woman who shows no discretion" (Proverbs 11:22 NIV).

It would be foolish to put a gold ring in a pig's nose in the same way it is foolish for a beautiful woman to not have discretion. The Amplified Bible expounds on the verse this way, "As a ring of gold in a swine's snout, so is a beautiful woman who is without discretion [her lack of character mocks her beauty]." A lack of discretion, or lack of good judgment, takes away from any outward beauty.

As I get older and my arms aren't as firm, as more wrinkles appear and my body isn't quite in the shape it once was, I must be careful where I allow my focus to go. I could become consumed by how I *used* to look or what size I *used* to wear. I have heard women talk about the attention that they *used* to be able to get from men. The heads they *used* to be able to turn. We've seen the shows and heard about the great lengths that woman go to just to remain beautiful in the eyes of the world.

Why do we do that? We can't keep up because the world's standard of beauty is always changing.

The Word says, "Charm is deceitful, and beauty is passing, but a woman who fears the Lord, she shall be praised" (Proverbs 31:30). If beauty is passing, then we must come to the place in our heart where we say, "God, I want to be beautiful from the inside out and beautiful for You."

More than anything in my life, at this point in my walk with the Lord, I want to know what He considers beautiful. I want to be beautiful to Jesus. I know that if I am beautiful to Him, I will be beautiful to others. We need to look to the Word to discover what God says real beauty is all about.

* * *

Several years ago, a friend of mine who worked at a local bank told me something about our daughter that I've never forgotten. Our daughter loves the Lord, and she has always had a tender heart for Him. One day she went into the bank to make a deposit. After she had left, the teller who waited on her leaned over to my friend and said, "That Sarah, she is beautiful inside and out and she doesn't even know it."

I was so blessed by the statement: "Beautiful inside and out and she doesn't even know it." What the bank teller saw was the Spirit of God living within her and the inner beauty that flows out from Him. The Word tells us:

> "Don't be concerned about the outward beauty of fancy hairstyles, expensive jewelry, or beautiful clothes. You should clothe yourselves instead with the beauty that comes from within, the unfading beauty of a gentle and quiet spirit, which is so precious to God." (1 Peter 3:3-4 NLT)

Beauty that comes from a gentle, quiet spirit is precious to God. Is a gentle, quiet spirit precious to the world? Not always. But are we living for the world or for God?

As we continue to age, I am certain that there will be times when we look in the mirror and wince at what our eyes see. But when our mind wants to begin to pick apart all the physical flaws, that is when we must turn our focus on what the Lord sees. Let's listen for that still, small voice that says, "You are altogether beautiful, my darling; there is no flaw in you" (Song of Solomon 4:7 NIV).

I love that Dove is choosing natural, everyday women to represent their brand, but it's time we refuse to allow the beauty industry to set our standard for what defines beauty. We change our identity when we allow God to set those standards for us. As we spend time before Him in prayer, let's ask Him to help us radiate the beauty of a gentle, quiet spirit before a world that knows anything but gentleness or quietness.

In the Dove commercial, I remember one little girl who said, "I will remind myself every day that I am beautiful." That is a good rule to live by. I would only add, "I will remind myself every day that God says I am beautiful, and He defines me."

Activate, Become, and Confess as you seek to change your identity one letter at a time.

## Activate – Start the Work

- Are you more concerned with outer beauty or inner beauty?
- How have you balanced the two in your life?
- How do you react when someone says you are beautiful?

## Become – Come into Existence and #beYOU

- What false beliefs about beauty do you want to do away with?
- Read 1 Peter 3:3–4 again. Notice it doesn't say hair and clothing and jewelry are bad; instead, it says those are the things we are not to be most concerned about. What steps will you take to live by God's beauty standard rather than the world's?

## Confess – Declare in Faith

By faith, I will no longer accept a false standard of beauty. I will allow the Lord to develop within me the incorruptible beauty of a gentle and quiet spirit. In Him I can be calm and self-controlled, not overanxious, but serene and spiritually mature. This is very precious in the sight of God, as am I (1 Peter 3:4, paraphrased).

## Let's pray:

Father, thank You for making me, me! Thank You for closing my eyes to the world's definition of beauty. Thank You for showing me where my heart has led me astray to believe beauty is defined by my outward looks and all that is inside didn't matter. It does matter, Lord. To You, it matters. How I speak to others matters; how I work and prioritize life and purpose matters. Grow within me a gentle and peaceful spirit, one that is calm and self-controlled. Help me to not be anxious for anything, but trusting in You alone, I will be at peace. That is when my true beauty will flow. Thank You, Jesus.

# C Is for *Changed*

## God says I am CHANGED.

The Spirit of the LORD will come powerfully
upon you, and you will prophesy with
them; and you will be *changed* into
a different person.

—1 Samuel 10:6 NIV, emphasis mine

**Change:** *to make radically different;
to replace with another.*[5]

When I first accepted that God could do a better job of running my life than I could, I know that I didn't give much thought to the changes He would make inside of me. I knew I needed *a* change but it didn't occur to me then that the truth was: *I* needed to change. If we are willing to be honest, we all have a tendency at times to blame others for the circumstances of our lives. I am no different. It was easy for me to blame everyone but me for my unhappiness. I arrogantly ignored the broken areas within and pointed fingers of blame to those around me. However, there were wrong perceptions, attitudes, deep wounds, and let's say "personality traits" God knew I needed to change. Others knew it, too.

There was just one catch to the process: I needed to allow Him access to my heart so He could begin revision on the areas He determined needed work. I also had to allow the people He brought into my life to be used as His tools of choice in the process of change—whether it was to speak a hard truth to me, bring the sting of correction, reveal my need for patience, or help me grow in loving others.

Proverbs 27:17 says, "As iron sharpens iron, so one person sharpens another" (NIV). Is it any wonder God uses others to grow us? People are often brought into our lives for a season and a purpose. Allowing them to sharpen us is an opportunity for growth. As they move in and out of our lives, we should ask God to show us His purpose for the relationship. I often ask myself if I am willing to give others permission to speak truth to me. Can I trust my friendships will help me grow? What change does God intend to happen within me as I do life with them?

One night many years ago, the Lord gave me a dream I vividly remember to this day; it was shortly after I sincerely surrendered my heart to Him. This was one of those dreams that is so real the details stick with you. In the dream, I was sitting at a picnic table surrounded by family and friends when a sudden wave of nausea hit me. Feeling sick to my stomach, I also began to sense what felt like a long string in my mouth. I reached with my right hand, grabbed the string, and with a strong tug pulled a boot out of my mouth.

Yes indeed, you read correctly—a boot! I pulled a big ol' boot from between my lips. But I wasn't done with a boot!

After a few minutes, I felt the same sensation, and when I pulled on the string again, this time a tin can emerged! This went on for some time as I sat at the picnic table pulling out items from within me: a tire, more tin cans, and many miscellaneous objects. Needless to say, it was very disturbing.

During this season of my life, the Lord had provided me with a Christian mentor, so I called her up and explained the dream. After a brief silence, she responded, "It sounds to me like you have a lot of junk inside of you and God wants to pull it out."

The sense of peace that washed over me confirmed to me her words were correct. I also knew I had a choice to make. Several options were before me. I could shut my mouth and refuse to allow God access to all that was inside of me. Or I could give Him access to certain areas of my life while keeping others off limits to Him. Or I could let Him have *all* of me. Every part of my heart could belong to Him, and I could give Him permission to change me.

I knew I had no choice. If I was to break free from my own torment, the only option for me was to surrender my heart completely to Him and let Him begin my transformation. My tears became my prayers to become the woman He had destined me to be, and His work began within my heart. He spoke to me through His Word, "I will give you a new heart and put a new spirit within you; I will take the heart of stone out of your flesh and give you a heart of flesh" (Ezekiel 36:26).

My cold, unhappy old heart that once held so much bitterness, anger, and resentment has been removed. In its place, He put a heart filled with compassion, love, and a desire for all God has for me. He has helped me see life from a different perspective—His!

In Ephesians 4, Paul tells us to let go of our old man and put on a new man:

> But you have not so learned Christ, if indeed you have heard Him and have been taught by Him, as the truth is in Jesus: that you put off, concerning your former conduct, the old man which grows corrupt according to the deceitful lusts, and be renewed in the spirit of your mind, and that you put on the new man which was created according to God, in true righteousness and holiness. (Ephesians 4:20-25)

When we latch on to faith and allow God to reshape our thinking we will become free to view ourselves the same way God does. His opinion is truth. What He says is true about me He says is true about you. God alone knows the full potential of others. Let's not limit what He can do. When voices around me try to convince me I will never change, I remind myself that change doesn't happen overnight. I will continue to change for the rest of my life here on earth. We need to close our ears to the lie that screams, "you will never change" or "they will never change."

Change is gradual and always possible. If God had required me to change everything overnight, I would have found myself in a heap of defeat. Let's allow God to work out the changes in each of His kids in His time, not ours. Let's not limit God with disbelief. When we present God with a surrendered heart, He can work miracles in our lives, and others will take notice. Spend time in His Word every day—get to know Him and His ways. I'm preaching to myself here too! Hebrews 4:12 says, "For the word of God is alive and powerful. It is sharper than the sharpest two-edged sword, cutting between soul and spirit, between joint and marrow. It exposes our innermost thoughts and desires" (NLT).

The Word is alive and has the power to change people. I can tell others about what God wants for them and what the Word of God says, but if there is no visible difference in me or I am not living out an active, life-changing faith, what good does it do for them? One of the greatest ways I can show others that God is capable of the change they long for is through the changes they see in me. Talk is cheap. It's easy to preach and tell others how they should live. It's a completely different story when we actually live it out. It's time to believe the Word can do what it says it can do and that we are who it says we are.

Our identity changes—one letter at a time—when we choose to allow the Lord's handiwork to transform us like a potter transforms clay. When this happens, you are no longer required to respond to situations in the way you have always done in the past. You can respond to people and circumstances as Christ would have you respond, because His Spirit lives inside of you. You no longer need to be controlled by emotions or by your enemies. You can walk in the power of the Holy Spirit and live for Christ—in victory. Each of us can choose to glorify Christ by our changed life.

Activate, Become, and Confess as you seek to change your identity one letter at a time.

## Activate – Start the Work

- Read Psalm 139 and use the words as a prayer to God.
- What did you discover about your true identity from this reading?

## Become – Come into Existence and #beYOU

- What false beliefs about yourself do you need to relinquish in order to step into your *changed* identity?
- What qualities of your old identity (before you knew Christ) creep back into your life sometimes? You can release those and start fresh by recommitting to God's work of transforming you into someone who looks like Him.

## Confess – Declare in Faith

I am changed because "I have been crucified with Christ; it is no longer I who live, but Christ lives in me; and the life which I now live in the flesh I live by faith in the Son of God, who loved me and gave Himself for me" (Galatians 2:20).

### *Let's pray:*

Father God, thank You so much for showing me who I can be. Thank You for changing me into the person You created me to be. Forgive me for believing the lie that says I can't change old habits and mindsets. Thank You for showing me that when I surrender to You and allow You to shape me, change happens. Thank You for changing me. Because of You, Jesus, I am changed! Amen.

# D Is for *Desired*

God says He DESIRES me.

Then the King will *desire* your beauty; Because
He is your Lord, bow down and honor Him.
—Psalm 45:11 AMP, emphasis mine

**Desire:** *something longed or hoped for, the feeling of wanting something; conscious impulse toward something that promises enjoyment or satisfaction in its attainment.*[6]

When I was a little girl, I used to dream about my wedding day. My pretend play always seemed to involve a wedding! On Sundays, if my best friend and I were able to convince our parents to allow us to spend the day together after church, we usually grabbed the bridal section in the Sunday newspaper and made plans for our someday weddings. The memory makes me laugh now as I remember how we would sit for the longest time gazing at the pictures of the brides and choosing which one we were going to look like when we were old enough to marry.

As a little girl, it was fun to daydream about the beautiful dress and the wedding that I would one day have. Every girl wants to feel like a princess, don't they? Of course, they do! Many of us love a fairy tale, me included.

As I grew into a young woman, the daydreams began to give way to a desire. I began to have a deep desire for that certain someone who would bring satisfaction and enjoyment to my life. I wanted a fairy-tale wedding to my Prince Charming. My personal fairy tale began when I started dating and then eventually became engaged to my Prince Charming, Pat. He was my high school sweetheart and the man I loved more than anything. After months (years, actually) of preparation and planning, I was finally a real bride. (I wonder if a little girl ever cut my picture out from the paper.)

Even though my wedding was several decades ago, I clearly remember the feelings I experienced as a bride. My heart held anticipation and excitement for our future together. So, one October day we met at the altar as two individuals and walked out of the church united together as one. My wedding day was one of the happiest days of my life. I felt like a princess, confident God had brought me my prince.

Our wedding was not quite as elaborate as a royal wedding. We gathered at a small church in Western New York and held a reception at the local fire hall. But the love of family and friends surrounded us, and we were excited to walk out the doors of that fire hall and into our future. We have now spent countless hours together through the years getting to know one another and learning to trust and understand each other.

It reminds me of a wedding in the Bible; this one, a true royal wedding. We have been given a promise in the Scriptures of the wedding of the Bridegroom, Jesus, with His radiant bride, His church. Someday Jesus is coming back for His bride, the bride of Christ, which is the church—those who have accepted His gift of salvation. Like the dreams of my own wedding as a girl, as Christians, we can now look forward to the day when Jesus returns and gathers His bride. As we hold desire in our hearts for the day we will marry our beloved, God has desire for us, and He wants us to prepare for that day.

The relationship between a bride and groom is incredibly intimate and is made physically tangible on the wedding day. Isaiah 62:5b says, "And as the bridegroom rejoices over the bride, so shall your God rejoice over you." When I attend a wedding, one of my favorite moments is watching the groom's expression as he views his bride for the first time. I will quickly look at her as she enters the room, but then my focus turns to the groom so I can watch his reaction to her entrance. There is a depth of emotion in his eyes, which I daresay one would have a hard time putting into words.

I've watched each of our own children look into the eyes of their spouse on their wedding day and I could see the joy, the anticipation, and the desire within them. When they stood and pledged their love to one another, they made a promise of commitment. The intimate looks they gave one another throughout the day spoke quietly and softly of the unspoken words of love for one another. Their love runs deep for one another, and in the same way, our Heavenly Father's love runs deep. He rejoices over us and has desire for us.

Take a moment and consider how lovingly He looks upon us. Note how tender He is and how precious we are to Him. Psalm 139:17 says, "How precious also are Your thoughts to me, O God! How great is the sum of them!" The Hebrew word for precious, *yaqar,* means "to esteem, be prized, be valuable, be precious, be costly, and be appraised."[7] Do you know what that means to you and me? You are a prize to God. I am a prize to God. We are His bride, and He is looking for us to be without "spot or wrinkle *or any such thing,* but that she should be holy and without blemish" (Ephesians 5:27, emphasis mine) as we prepare ourselves for His return.

There have been so many times when I was not able to view myself as a prize, and I've certainly never seen myself as a valuable, precious prize. The truth is some days I don't feel that I am all that desirable. In fact, there are moments when I can be just plain ugly. Whenever I allow my feelings to control my attitude and actions, I become pretty undesirable. Oh, how I despise that ugly side of me.

Miraculously, I have married a man with the gift of grace. He's a man who has loved me on my good days and through all my bad ones. I see the Spirit of God in him because I know that somehow God, too, looks past the ugliness and still sees the desirable me—the one He desires to use to glorify Him.

Not only does God desire a relationship with me, but He also wants that relationship to be an intimate one. When I first became a Christian, I would often hear messages suggesting I become intimate with the Lord, and I would wonder how that was possible. Well, as I look back on thirty-plus years of marriage, I am now able to understand it better. I can see how the intimacy with my husband has increased through each year as we continue to grow closer. We have endured both good and bad times together and now experience a deeper level of commitment than we did on our wedding day. My desire is for my husband alone. I would never want to hurt him in any way. In fact, I love to be a blessing to him.

If someone had told me on my wedding day that the love I had for Pat at that moment would be *the least* amount I'd have for him, I never would have believed them. But it's true. Every day I spend with him, my love grows deeper. And just as the love for my husband has grown through the years, so has my love for the Lord. As I have spent time in His Word learning about Him and getting to know Him, I have a deeper understanding and a much more intimate relationship with Him. The wonder for me is that God *desires* that intimate relationship too.

For some, it can be hard to believe that God would find us desirable enough to *want* to be intimate with us. We tend to replay our shameful moments; we remind ourselves of what we've done—or maybe what was done *to* us—circumstances we might view as so damaging and dirty that it is almost impossible to imagine we could be the pure and spotless bride for whom Jesus is coming back. But, my friend, this is the beauty of the cross on which Jesus suffered and died for us.

David cried out to God after his sin with Bathsheba was revealed: "Purify me from my sins, and I will be clean; wash me, and I will be whiter than snow" (Psalm 51:7 NLT). I love the way The Message Bible states the same verse, "Soak me in your laundry and I'll come out clean, scrub me and I'll have a snow-white life" (Psalm 51:7 MSG). Oh, how good God is to us. We begin to change our identity when we determine we will hold back nothing from Him. He desires our time, our love, our devotion, our hearts, our thoughts, our relationships, and our dreams. Just as a new bride and her bridegroom spend countless hours getting to know one another, in a more intimate way, Christ, our Bridegroom, desires the same.

Activate, Become, and Confess as you seek to change your identity one letter at a time.

## Activate – Start the Work

- Read Matthew 25:1-13. What does Jesus want you to know from this passage?
- How should the bride for Christ prepare for her wedding?
- How does it make you feel to know God desires you and wants a relationship with you?

## Become – Come into Existence and #beYOU

- Are there issues from your past that hinder your ability to believe that God would desire an intimate relationship with you? If so, pray for His truth to override any feelings of doubt; He longs for you to step into your *desired* identity as the bride of Christ.

## Confess – Declare in Faith

I am the bride of Christ! I am desired by my Bridegroom, Jesus. I will rejoice and shout for joy as I prepare for the royal wedding celebration. I will give Him the glory and honor He deserves, as I remain faithful to my Groom. (Revelation 19:7, paraphrased).

## Let's pray:

Father, I ask You to take me to a deeper level of intimacy in our relationship. Lord, I know I can't hide anything from You, so I give You my past and my pain; I surrender my shame and my sorrow to You, God. Set me free from the lies that have kept me from believing You could ever befriend me, much less desire me. Help me, Lord, to live every day confident that You, God, desire me regardless of anything I have done or said. I give You permission to move in my life and to take me as deep as You desire for me to go. Amen.

# E Is for *Established*

God says He has ESTABLISHED my steps.

> I waited patiently for the LORD; And He
> inclined to me, And heard my cry.
> He also brought me up out of a horrible
> pit, Out of the miry clay, And set my feet upon
> a rock, And *established* my steps.
> —Psalm 40:1–2, emphasis mine

**Establish:** *to make firm or stable.*[8]

I have a confession. I am not a patient person. I would love to say that you could look up the word *patient* in the dictionary and my name would be next to it, but that would not happen. Due to my lack of patience, I have set out on many journeys to fulfill my purpose only to discover that my steps were either out of God's timing or I had totally missed the mark. It's simple for me to recognize *now* that much of my life has been striving—in my own strength—to make my will be God's will.

As a new Christian desperate to discover God's will for my life, I was eager to do great things for the Lord. I'd been told, "Dream big dreams because nothing is impossible with God." So, I did. But when the wait was too long, or I had a thought that seemed like something God could be in—zoom! I was off and running with or without God.

Unfortunately, stepping out before God meant attempting to move mountains in my own strength and timing. When the outcome didn't match my plan, when the dream collapsed and failure followed, the three d's became my constant companions: disappointment, discouragement and depression. Thankfully, for what I lack in patience, the Lord has a generous supply to give. When the road I was on brought me to Psalm 40, I could offer it as my own personal prayer. There are hard times of striving and there are lonely times of waiting; I can now see that God leaves the striving to me, but He is always in the waiting.

In Psalm 40:1, the translation from Hebrew for "I waited patiently" would literally be "waiting I waited."[9] *Waiting . . . I waited*—I just can't get over that. I absolutely love David's heart; there is so much we can learn from him. I'm not sure what trouble he was going through at the time he wrote this psalm, but I know he was a man who understood trouble. He walked through plenty of hard times, and through each trial he faced, he always found that he needed to rely solely on God for his supply.

God called David "a man after His own heart" (1 Samuel 13:14). Yet, he still was a man—a human just like you and me—who fell into troubled times during his life. Every time David cried out for the Lord's help, He was there to meet him. In the first verse of Psalm 40, David wrote that the Lord "inclined to me," which makes me think of the moments I've been inclined to turn toward my child when they released a cry for help. Most parents move quickly when they hear their own child's unmistakable cry for help. And like a child waiting to be rescued, David tells us that while he was waiting for God to move, he just waited. And he did so *patiently*.

David patiently waited; the Lord heard his cry, and He bent down toward him and lifted him out of the abominable pit he was in. It was his time in the pit that drew him closer to God. If we keep our eyes focused on God rather than our circumstance, our time in the pit will draw us closer, as well. However, if you are anything like me, being stuck in the mire (something like quicksand) is not all that appealing.

Oh, I have spent some time there. I may not have been physically stuck in the mud—well, truth be told, I actually *have* found myself stuck in some mud a few times, but that's not the kind of mud I'm talking about. I'm talking about the place when life is messy and you feel suffocated and buried beneath the pain of it.

I've been there, and I've believed I might die there.

Many times throughout the years, I anticipated God answering my prayers a certain way, and when the answer was different, I was crushed. Then I would allow my two pity-party friends, Hurt and Disappointment, to take me by the hand and lead me deeper into my muddy mess. "Come and sit over here for a spell," they seemed to whisper.

Once I was there, climbing back out seemed too great a feat to accomplish. In fact, once a minister I had never met before prayed for me and he said, "Hope deferred makes the heart sick." That was a perfect description of me—heartsick over every deferred hope. At the time he spoke those words to me, I was extremely busy trying to make my will be God's will. I was misinterpreting Psalm 37:4, which tells us God will give us the desires of our heart. I thought the verse meant God would say yes to every desire I had. I did not fully understand that as I made God my delight and became more concerned about His desires than mine, He would put His desires within me. I also needed to learn how to trust His "no."

Now I understand it doesn't work that way. But back then I was extremely selfish—everything needed to happen on my terms. In fact, at the time, my husband had a sweet little nickname for me, "Mrs. One-way." It was difficult for me to accept a *no* from anyone (including the Lord) when I had my heart and mind set on a matter—especially when I was certain the answer should be yes. Then, when my hopes fell apart, so did I. I was like a two-year-old having a temper tantrum.

Have you ever felt as though maybe physically you weren't walking in "mire" but you were going through something that made you feel as though you might as well be? Every step feels heavy, defeated, and completely unbearable. I'm certain most of us have experienced the metaphysical *pit* at one time or another, but God never intended for that to become our dwelling place. How do we escape?

After the Lord bent toward David, He reached down, lifted David out of the pit of destruction; He set his feet on a rock, and established his steps. When I read this, I just have to stop and spend a few moments giving thanks. What a promise of hope! God will reach down and put me on a rock. Interestingly enough, one of the words translated from Hebrew for *rock* is ". . . as stronghold of Jehovah, of security."[10] I believe this is an accurate description of God. God is referred to as a *Rock* in

34

Scripture. He wants to reach down and pull me out of the pit I am in and set me upon Himself—upon the Rock of His Word, upon the Rock of His foundation and truth. Once I realized that the Word was the ladder that would help me climb out of the pit and walk securely, determined, and steadfast, I began to devour each word.

We all spend time in miscellaneous pits. The pit that leads to destruction can look like the pit of depression, or it might be a pit of fear and insecurity. There are pits of alcoholism and drug abuse, pits of pornography and sexual addiction, or pits of discouragement and despair. There are pits of low self-esteem and the pits of past regrets. The pits of jealousy and envy aren't much fun. I have spent a good share of my time in each of those pits.

We have all walked through episodes from our past that can leave scars. Those scars will become chains that bind us to the wall of the pit if we don't break free from them. God says, "For I know the thoughts that I think toward you, says the Lord, thoughts of peace and not of evil, to give you a future and a hope" (Jeremiah 29:11). In the same way He intended it for His children of Israel in this verse, God never intended for us to reside in our pits. His plan was for each of His kids to live full of hope, walking the steps He alone established. He wants us to trust His healing process and do the work that's necessary to get out of any pit to which we become confined.

As I considered this verse and talked to the Lord about it, I thought about the decisions I have made throughout my life. I also thought about the pits I have allowed myself to dwell in. I can see now that some steps were definitely established by Him—and other steps, well, not so much. I also came to understand how different circumstances affect our time in the pit. Sometimes I found myself in the pit not because of my decisions but the decisions and choices of others. But I also spent some time in the pit as consequence for my own bad choices.

There were times I was in the pit because I have an enemy, and his name is Satan. He is a schemer, and his desire is to destroy me. Yet, regardless of why I might have been in the pit, I know the Lord never wanted me there. He wants us to get out, and He is willing to reach down and help pull us out. But what is our part? David wrote that as he was crying out for help, the Lord "heard his cry" (Psalm 40:1). If we are ever going to get out of the pit and walk the established steps God has for us, the first step is to cry out to Him for help.

When David asked God to lift him out of the pit and he began walking the steps God had established for him, he was given another gift. The Lord put a new song in his mouth—a song that would change the lives of others. How? Instead of a man pressed by the pit, they would see God's glory through the changes in David's appearance. The changes in one person can be the catalyst for another to seek the Lord for their own release from the pit. We change our identity when we understand this is what God wants for each of us: to sing a new song, a song of hope, a song of freedom, a song of worship that shows others that you can overcome the pit, a song that shows others they do not belong in a pit but on established steps.

The Lord has prepared steps for each one of us to take to fulfill His plan for our lives and ultimately bring Him glory. They may look different than we think. In fact, they almost always do. I took a great big U-turn when I began walking in His steps, and my life is far better now than I could ever have imagined it to be.

Activate, Become, and Confess as you seek to change your identity one letter at a time.

## Activate - Start the Work

- Your first step is to recognize your pit. What consumes your thoughts and conversations? What makes you feel as though you could never break free from it?
- One place to start is to confess that struggle to God. Then it's time to repent, release, and renew. Repent means to turn around and go in a new direction. Describe what your life could look like if you got "unstuck" and went in a new direction.

## Become – Come into Existence and #beYOU

- Ponder this: "For those who are living according to the flesh set their minds on the things of the flesh [which gratify the body], but those who are living according to the Spirit, [set their minds on] the things of the Spirit [His will and purpose]" (Romans 8:5 AMP).
- Where do you set your mind? Is your focus on you or on God?
- What steps do you think will help you change your focus?
- How do you feel about God being a Rock on which you can take steady steps on a path He *established* for you?

## Confess – Declare in Faith

I will wait patiently for You, Lord. I trust that You will lean Your ear to me and hear my cry. You will lift me up out of a horrible pit, out of the mess I feel trapped in, and set my feet upon a rock. You have established steps for me to walk. I will sing the new song You have for me so loudly that others will see it and trust in You (Psalm 40:1–3, paraphrased).

## Let's pray:

Father God, thank You for the good plan You have for me. I am thankful that You have established steps for me, and even though I have wandered away from them, You can guide me back to them. Oh Father, I want to be free from this pit. The muddy mess I have found myself in has prevented me from singing the song You have placed within me. I acknowledge my sin to You. The sin of [name it] has entangled me. I want out. I want freedom. I want to sing the new song—the song of freedom. Help me to patiently wait as You bring me back to the steps You've established for me, Lord. I pray in Jesus's name. Amen.

# F Is for *Forgiven*

God says He has FORGIVEN me.

If we confess our sins, He is faithful and just
to *forgive* us our sins and to cleanse us
from all unrighteousness.

—1 John 1:9, emphasis mine

**Forgive:** *to cease to feel resentment against; to give up resentment of or claim to requital; to grant relief from payment of.*[11]

I prayed relentlessly for God to reveal the word for the letter F—I couldn't decide between *forgiveness* and *freedom*. I continued to debate between the two, but eventually the Lord helped me realize both words actually go hand in hand. He reminded me that when you have found true forgiveness through Christ, you can walk in freedom. When we find the forgiveness that Christ offers, it helps us live free from guilt, condemnation, the regrets of the past, and even our present mistakes and challenges. As we learn to accept and receive Christ's forgiveness, we can then come to a place of learning how to forgive others and ourselves. Forgiveness provides freedom from the bondage of holding on to grudges or carrying bitterness within our hearts.

Have you met someone imprisoned by the grudges they harbor against another? Ever known someone full of bitterness and resentment? I have—me! I'm not proud of it, but I used to be full of both. Holding on to a grudge was like my job! It was a very high-paying job, too. But eventually, I realized I was the one paying. It was costing me a great deal, and I wasn't reaping any benefits from it, either! Well, other than a bitter, resentful, hateful heart, and several broken relationships, but I wouldn't call those benefits. I was not very fun to be around. I'm extremely grateful that I am no longer that person. And I never need to go back to being her.

Sometimes I struggled with wrongs done against me. Other times, it was the sins of my past that would torment me on an almost daily basis. Offering forgiveness to anyone may feel worse than physical torture to you, but living in perpetual blame is, ultimately, far worse. We convince ourselves that we don't need to forgive because, after all, it is within our rights to hold on to that grudge. But when we focus on our "righteous" anger, we forget just how much we've been forgiven. We keep mental records of wrongs done to us, overlooking that we could never stand a chance if the Lord kept record of all our sins.

If You, Lord, should keep an account of our sins
and treat us accordingly, O Lord, who could stand
[before you in judgment and claim innocence]?
(Psalm 130:3 AMP)

Who could stand? No one. Not you, and certainly not me.
When we refuse to reach out and extend forgiveness to
others, we presume that what has been done to us is somehow
far worse than anything we could have done. When Peter asked
Jesus how many times we should forgive someone who sins
against us, Jesus responded: not seven times, but up to seventy
times seven (Matthew 18:21–22). Peter probably thought he
was being generous with his suggestion of seven times. Jesus
must've thrown his generosity off kilter with His point that we
shouldn't keep count at all but always be willing to forgive.

There is a beautiful story found in Luke 7 about a woman
who found freedom after realizing just how much she had been
forgiven. This woman entered the home where Jesus was and
brought her alabaster flask of fragrant oil; she began washing
the feet of Jesus with her tears as she anointed Him with the oil.
Simon, one of the Pharisees, looked on with disgust, believing
that if Jesus really was a prophet, He would know what she
was—a sinner.

The Pharisee in this story thought his sins could never compare with the sins of the woman. He believed himself to be
superior and her sins to be far greater than his own. However,
I've never seen anything in the Scriptures of God placing our
sins in degrees of "wrongness." I just know I've allowed pride
to cause me to judge like the Pharisee. Jesus says that if we are
forgiven much, we love much (Luke 7:47). I did not love much
because I had the mindset that my sin wasn't as bad or as serious as someone else's might be. I did not understand that no
matter what sin I commit, when I sin against God's laws, I sin

41

against Him. There is no escaping the fact that "all have sinned and fall short of the glory of God" (Romans 3:23).

Sitting at the feet of Jesus, this woman, who was bruised and broken by a lifestyle of sin, saw the freedom that forgiveness would bring to her life, and she was willing to pour out everything she had of value upon Him. It's only arrogance that makes me believe I don't need to get on my knees before the Lord, break open my "alabaster box," and pour out my heart of thanks to Him for all I have been forgiven.

The beauty of finding forgiveness through Christ's loving sacrifice is that no matter what we have done, there is no longer a need to be tormented by our sins. When we are sincere and ask for His forgiveness from our sins, He freely grants it. He does not hold our sins against us like most humans would; in fact, He removes them "as far as the east is from the west, so far has He removed our transgressions from us" (Psalm 103:12). For all who come to Him with a truly repentant heart, He forgives them. Psalm 86:5 says, "For You, Lord, are good, and ready to forgive, and abundant in mercy to all those who call upon You." He's always ready to forgive.

Aren't you so thankful for that promise? I know I am! He has always been ready to forgive, but it is up to us to ask.

The next question is: then what? What comes after forgiveness?

Freedom! When we know without any doubt that our sins have been forgiven, it is absolutely possible to walk in freedom. "Because of the sacrifice of the Messiah, his blood poured out on the altar of the Cross, we're a free people—free of penalties and punishments chalked up by all our misdeeds. And not just barely free, either; abundantly free" (Ephesians 1:7–10 MSG). We are free to let go of bitterness, resentment, and hurt. We don't need to hold on to the ugly grudges we bear.

Freedom came into my heart the day that I decided to let go of all the resentments I held against those who hurt me. I live in freedom every moment I choose to refuse the invitation to irritation's party and no longer allow myself to get mad over every little, or big, thing!

While watching the movie *For Richer or Poorer*,[12] the Lord used a scene with Tim Allen and a horse to drop a spiritual truth into my heart. The Lord does creative things like that. Tim's character was trying to get the horse to plow the field, and when the horse refused to follow directions, his frustration led him to speak unkindly to the horse. After a moment, he encouraged the horse to forgive him with a simple suggestion: "Let it go. Just let it go."

As soon as I saw it, I felt a knowing within my heart. This was exactly what the Lord wanted me to do. This is how I would discover the freedom that comes from letting things go and brushing off offenses and irritations. He also revealed to me that I am free when I don't blame others for my mistakes or make excuses when I sin or fall short of God's expectations. Christ helped me realize that when I dwell on wrongs done to me, the pain of resentment shoves me right back into prison. Freedom brings joy and peace.

We change our identity and live as forgiven when we choose the freedom of forgiveness. When we can acknowledge how much we have been forgiven and freely offer the same gift to others, we will find our freedom. The one who the Son sets free is free indeed (John 8:36). Don't return to bondage.

Activate, Become, and Confess as you seek to change your identity one letter at a time.

## Activate - Start the Work

- Is there someone you need to forgive? Whose name comes to mind?

- Do you struggle with forgiving yourself? What thing do you think is "so bad" that God couldn't forgive you?
- Ask the Lord to show who you need to forgive to activate forgiveness in your life.
- Ask Him to help you to forgive yourself so you can be released from that bondage.

## Become – Come into Existence and #beYOU

- Hebrews 11:1 says, "Now faith is confidence in what we hope for and assurance about what we do not see" (NIV). Believing that God can and will forgive our sins requires faith. Do you have faith deep enough to believe it?
- If not, what do you think hinders your faith and holds you back from receiving forgiveness?
- What would help you to have the confidence to believe you can be forgiven?

## Confess – Declare in Faith

It is absolutely clear that God has called me to a free life. However, I will not use this freedom as an excuse to do whatever I want to do. Doing so will destroy my freedom—never gain it. Rather, I will use the freedom Christ provided for me to serve others in love. This is how God's Word is summed up: Love others as you love yourself. That's an act of true freedom (Galatians 5:13-14, paraphrased).

## Let's pray:

Oh Father, I know I am only a sinner saved by Your grace. Help me to overcome any resentment I hold in my heart toward others—even against myself. Please help me to forgive others as You have forgiven me. Help me to release any injustice against me into Your capable hands, Lord. I pour out my pain on You now, Lord; I pour out all that I hold dear to me, all that I possess; I pour it out to You and ask for You to take this hurt [name the hurt], I give you this resentment [name the resentment] toward [name of person]. I release it now, in Jesus's name. Thank You that I can now walk in the fullest form of freedom that forgiveness brings. Amen.

# G Is for *God's Child*

God says I am His CHILD.

But as many as received Him, to them He gave
the right to become *children of God*,
to those who believe in His name.

—John 1:12 NIV, emphasis mine

**Father:** *a man who exercises paternal
care over other persons; paternal
protector or provider.*[13]

When I was seven years old, my parents adopted an adorable little girl from Korea. She was ten months old when she arrived, and her name was Park Sun Duk. I can still recall the excitement stirring inside of me when it was time to go to the airport and retrieve my new baby sister. After months of waiting, it felt as though the day would never happen; now, it was finally here. There was such joy on my mom's face when she was handed this sweet, beautiful baby girl that she could now call her own.

Two years later we welcomed a Korean boy, who was my age, named Chai Byung Lim. We did not go as a family to the airport to pick up my brother. My dad went this time while the rest of the family waited anxiously for his arrival at the house. Waiting for my dad to pull into the driveway was like watching grass grow! It seemed to take forever, but eventually the car pulled in, and out popped this cute little boy to a new life in a new home with his adopted family.

I do not recall every detail my parents went through as far as paperwork and finances to legally adopt these two children into our family. I do know, however, that once my parents first laid their eyes on each of their pictures in the packet, they wanted them. They loved them at first glance, and they were committed to adopting them and making them their children—legally. There was a process to make this happen and they committed to go through that process of filling out paperwork, having home visits, and getting the finances in order to make the dream a reality. They knew there were children who needed loving homes, and they desired to become parents of two of them in the hopes they would have a better life.

When asked how many children my parents had, the answer was always five. It was never "three natural and two adopted." They considered each one their child, regardless of how we arrived. It was never a concern to us that the color of our hair or the shapes of our eyes were different. We were brothers and sisters, and we fought like brothers and sisters do, too. We were now a complete family of five who all shared the same last name. My parents took pride in their kids, and like most parents, they would spend their days working to provide for and protect each one.

Just as people reach out and open their hearts and homes to adopt children to complete their families, God has also reached out and opened His heart so He could complete His. He is the inventor of adoption. God had His children the Israelites, and yet He saw that His family was not complete. He knew our need for Him, too. He knew that we needed a way of salvation, so He provided it. "But when the right time came, God sent his Son, born of a woman, subject to the law. God sent him to buy freedom for us who were slaves to the law, so that he could adopt us as his very own children" (Galatians 4:4–5 NLT). In the same way there was a cost for my parents to adopt my siblings, there was a cost to God; it was His Son.

Now, let me ask you this. What good does it do for a couple to go through the process of adoption only to have the child never acknowledge them as their parent? What would life have been like if my brother or sister never accepted our parents' last name or engaged in family life? They would have been disconnected and unfamiliar with the family. Those who are adopted need to receive and accept the love poured out to them from their new family. They also need to believe that everything that belongs to the parents now belongs to them.

In the same way, God says that "to all who believed him and accepted him, he gave the right to become children of God" (John 1:12 NIV). It's the receiving and believing on Jesus that allows us to become a child of God. Through faith in His Son, we have the legal right to share in His inheritance because we have been adopted as sons and daughters. The apostle Paul tells us, "In Him also we have obtained an inheritance, being predestined according to the purpose of Him who works all things according to the counsel of His will, that we who first trusted in Christ should be to the praise of His glory" (Ephesians 1:11–12). I like reminding myself that I am God's child.

There was another bonus my brother and sister received when they came to our home; they now had a father to defend them. And so do we. As God's children, we have a heavenly Father there to defend us. How tremendous it is for us that even when some of our earthly fathers fail to protect and defend their children, we have a heavenly Father who will never fail.

Years ago, I volunteered at our children's elementary school as the PTA president. One year, the committee and I needed to make an unpopular decision regarding the programming we had sponsored. One area in particular was the dance program, when the school principal had asked us to find a new dance teacher. As you can imagine, this did not go over very well with some of the parents who did not want a change. I received many cranky phone calls and heard rampant rumors. Anxiety began to fill me after hearing through the rumor mill that the next PTA meeting was going to be full of irate parents. Truthfully, I was petrified! I began to prepare my speech and gather all my information so I could be ready to defend myself.

While sitting at a stop light one morning and mentally going through my meeting agenda and defending myself to the Lord, I had a thought run through my mind. It was more than a thought, however, it was a statement that I knew the Lord dropped into my mind. I heard, "Jesus stood before Pontius Pilate and never spoke a word."

Hmm, it was an interesting moment for me when the truth of that statement settled within me. I was so worried I had to defend myself, it had never occurred to me that I could trust God to work the situation out. I had never asked Him to be my Defender before, but I realized at that moment how badly I needed Him to be that. Psalm 59:1 became my battle cry: "Deliver me from my enemies, O my God; defend me from those who rise up against me." You know what? It worked. Regardless of the grapevine threats I had heard, not one irate person came to the meeting that night. It was truly amazing to witness, and it continues to amaze me every time God shows Himself to be faithful as my Defender; claiming Him as such is part of my rightful inheritance in Him.

My brother and sister received new names the day my parents signed the paperwork to adopt them. They now had American names. They became citizens of the United States and they also became entitled to the inheritance my parents would set aside for their children one day. We, too, receive a new name, a new citizenship, and an inheritance when we commit to follow Christ; we become children of God. Philippians 3:20 says "our citizenship is in heaven, from which we also eagerly wait for the Savior, the Lord Jesus Christ." We have a great inheritance through Christ; not only have we inherited eternal life, we also have inherited the promises of His Word.

He is Father and Defender, regardless of the troubles we face in this life. He wants to fight for us. "But you, God, see the trouble of the afflicted; you consider their grief and take it in hand. The victims commit themselves to you; you are the helper of the fatherless" (Psalm 10:14 NIV).

You change your identity when you receive God as your Heavenly Father, confirming you are now His child. Your adoption papers have been signed and sealed, and He has a wonderful inheritance for you. Allow Him to be your Defender and Helper—and most importantly, your loving Father.

Activate, Become, and Confess as you seek to change your identity one letter at a time.

## Activate - Start the Work

- What was your relationship like with your father (or father figures in your life)?
- How does this relationship affect your view of God as a loving, protective Father? Describe whether it hinders or helps your understanding of God.
- What feelings do you have when you think of God as an adoptive Father?

## Become – Come into Existence and #beYOU

- Read Galatians 3:26–29. What does it say about how you can become a child of God?
- According to verse 28, what does this adoption change for us? What does that knowledge mean for you personally?
- Based on what verse 29 says, what does it mean to you to belong to Christ, be a descendant of Abraham, and an heir in God's big family?
- What pattern of thinking do you need to change to be who God says you are?

## Confess – Declare in Faith

What manner of love the Father has bestowed on me, that I should be called His child! The world will never understand me, because it did not know Him (1 John 3:1). He is my loving Father and my Defender. He loves me unconditionally as His child.

## *Let's pray:*

Father God, I admit there are many times I forget to think of myself as Your child and fail to allow You to be my Defender and Helper. But I acknowledge You today as my Father; I receive and trust You as a loving Father. I am Your child and, therefore, receive all that You have to give me. I am a co-heir with Christ and want to receive all the benefits You have for me as Your heir. I choose to live my life as Your adopted child, Lord. Help me to live in a way that honors You, Father, and our relationship. Amen!

# H Is for *Holy*

God says I am HOLY.

For I am the LORD who brings you up out of
the land of Egypt, to be your God. You shall
therefore be *holy,* for I am holy.

—Leviticus 11:45, emphasis mine

**Holy:** *religious and morally good; set
apart for the service of God or of a
divine being; having a divine quality.*[14]

One quiet morning as I was reading from the book of Leviticus, my eyes scanned across verse forty-five in chapter eleven, and a wave of shock washed over me. Reading the verse again, I looked up from my Bible and thought, "Lord, You expect me to be what? Holy as You are holy? That's impossible; *You* are Holy but I am not!" There was no doubt in my mind that Kolleen Lucariello looked nothing like the image of holiness I had flowing through my mind.

However, I could not get that one verse out of my mind. It continued to frequent my thoughts several times a day after reading it. The idea of being holy seems like such an outrageous request for God to make of His people, doesn't it? But why would God make such a request if it were impossible to complete? Would God set us up for failure like that? I just couldn't imagine it. That's when I began to ask Him for answers to this question: Is it really possible for us to be holy, as You are holy, Lord?

My quest for answers started by taking a closer look in Leviticus and the words to His chosen people, the Israelites. I began by considering God's laws and what He expected from them. If He expected them to follow His laws, would He expect any less from me? In this moment I realized I spent most of my time asking Him what I should *do* with my life, rather than how He wanted me to *live* my life. Questions began to rise within me . . .

- What changes would I need to make to live my life according to His laws?
- What would I personally look like if I were to live my life holy, as He is holy?
- How would I speak, think, and behave?
- How would I react to life's circumstances if I were to react out of a heart of holiness rather than my before-I-knew-Christ responses?

- Was He making a wishful statement, or did He mean that we actually could be holy?

This request seemed so unrealistic, but the more I learned about God, the more I realized that He gave us His Word as instruction—for our own good. He would not tell us to "be holy" as He is holy and not expect us to make every effort to obey those words. As hard as it was to understand, I knew I had my answer. He gave us His Word with every intention that we would pursue a life of holiness for Him. But I also felt strongly that He would never call us to a life of holiness and not give us the tools necessary to enable us in that pursuit.

So, if I were to pursue a life of holiness for the Lord, what changes would I need to make? Looking through the Old Testament and His laws gave me a pretty good understanding as to what I shouldn't do—He made that fairly clear. Through my seeking, I began to see how easy it could be to compromise His Word because of poor teaching, a lack of understanding, and the enticement for what the world has to offer. Many times I would intentionally try to negotiate God's will, and at other times I simply did not have a correct interpretation of what the Bible had to say on a matter. If we don't spend much time reading it, how can we? And when I did read, I felt I did not grasp its truth.

It was a shock when I discovered Leviticus 5:17. "If a person sins, and commits any of these things which are forbidden to be done by the commandments of the Lord, though he does not know it, yet he is guilty and shall bear his iniquity." Yikes! We are still held accountable for sin even if we do not recognize it as such. Using the excuse "I didn't know it was wrong" isn't going to matter. It was a great revelation to me when I discovered I could know His will for my life simply by reading His instruction manual (the Bible). If we resolve to take the time to search out the Bible, God will share His heart quite openly to reveal His desire for us on how we should live.

For example, in 1 Thessalonians 4:3 Paul shares, "God's will is for you to be holy," and then he goes on to say one way we can accomplish this is to "stay away from all sexual sin" (NLT). This is one of those areas of compromise to the world. Our culture and the media would lead us to believe that we own our bodies, and we can do whatever we want, do it however we want to, and do it with whomever we want. Well, that may be what the world wants us to believe, but God tells us differently.

God never intended for the world to set our moral compass for us. He set up boundaries for our protection and His glory. "God has called us to live holy lives, not impure lives. Therefore, anyone who refuses to live by these rules is not disobeying human teaching but is rejecting God, who gives his Holy Spirit to you" (1 Thessalonians 4:7–8 NLT).

Excuse-making was a big area of compromise for me. Too many times I allowed these thoughts to control my thinking: "It's too hard. I don't want people to think I am strange. What will my friends and family think?" Another phrase I used a lot was: "I am only human." While it is true—I am only human—in the end it really is just another great excuse to persist in sin. However, if I continued to believe the lie that I could stay in sin because I was, after all, "only human," then I would never be able to stop myself from any form of temptation.

These thoughts seemed to always pop up—front and center—whenever I had a conflict between what *I* wanted and what I knew *God* wanted. But I was introduced to a great verse in one of my very first Bible studies, and it has continued to help me through the years to overcome the battle with temptation.

Paul wrote to the Corinthian church, "The temptations in your life are no different from what others experience. And God is faithful. He will not allow the temptation to be more than you can stand. When you are tempted, he will show you a way out so that you can endure" (1 Corinthians 10:13 NLT). I need to be willing to run for the exit door when given the chance to do so. We all do. If we train ourselves to listen to our inner man (Ephesians 3:16), which is the Spirit *within* us, He will show us how to escape from the temptations *around* us.

Several years ago, my husband's company hosted a clambake for all the employees and families. It was held shortly after we had started to attend church, and we were learning more about God and His ways. We had begun to make some necessary changes in our lives that would help us live more in accordance with His Word. We planned to enjoy the party and the food, and I thought it might be a nice way to get to know some of his coworkers—many of whom I had never met. I hadn't given one thought to the alcohol that would be available to everyone. Alcohol has never been a great temptation for me. Surrounded by a group of Pat's coworkers, who stood in circle chatting, one of the ladies looked at me and said, "Kolleen, where is your drink?"

I replied, "Oh, I am fine, thank you. I'm okay with my soda."

I was caught off guard by her next comment, when she sarcastically said, "Do you realize how stupid you look standing there without a drink? We all have drinks, and you are the only one who doesn't. You look really dumb."

I was humiliated in front of people I did not even know; in fact, I really didn't even know this woman. It was the first time we had met face to face; she just worked with my husband. After her comment, the battle within me began as I fought the temptation to go and grab a cup of alcohol so I could look like everyone else. I also fought tears.

But, standing before the group, I realized this was my introduction to living my life differently than others. Not better than, just different than. I was standing in the middle of my first test of faith, and I could cave to the pressure or move beyond my fear of what others think. It was time for me to care more about what He thought because I was about to discover a life pleasing to God is a life set apart for Him.

I guess I have found my answer. God reveals His will for us is to live in holiness, but He doesn't stop there; He also will help us with the follow-through. If you're ready to go, "roll up your sleeves, put your mind in gear, be totally ready to receive the gift that's coming when Jesus arrives. Don't lazily slip back into those old grooves of evil, doing just what you feel like doing. You didn't know any better then; you do now. As obedient children, let yourselves be pulled into a way of life shaped by God's life, a life energetic and blazing with holiness. God said, 'I am holy; you be holy'" (1 Peter 1:13–16 MSG).

Changing our identity is going to require us to roll up our sleeves and refuse to become lazy in our habits. Decide to move into a life that pleases the One who matters most—Jesus.

Activate, Become, and Confess as you seek to change your identity one letter at a time.

## Activate - Start the Work

- Look up the word *holy* in a thesaurus. What are some synonyms listed that stand out to you?
- Of these words, pick one and do a word study on it through the Scriptures. Journal how God speaks to your heart as you do the work.

## Become – Come into Existence and #beYOU

- What excuses have you used to convince yourself that following God's will is too hard?

- Read Ephesians 5:10. What does this verse instruct you to do? How will you do that? Who will you seek out if you need help?
- What is your next step that will help you to become more like God's character?

## Confess – Declare in Faith

By the mercies of God, I will dedicate all of myself as a living sacrifice to God. It is my desire to honor and glorify God by becoming holy and pleasing to Him. This will be my intentional act of worship to Him (Romans 12:1, paraphrased). This is who I am: set apart, holy, and pleasing to God!

### Let's pray:

Father God, thank You for the reminder that nothing is too difficult for You to accomplish; that means my walking in holiness, as You have requested, is not too difficult for me. Thank You for the help You provide through the power of the Holy Spirit to make my life one pleasing to You. Amen.

# I Is for *Image*

God says I am made in His IMAGE.

So God created man in his own *image*, in
the *image* of God he created him;
male and female he created them.
—Genesis 1:27, emphasis mine

**Image:** *a physical likeness or
representation of a person, animal,
or thing, photographed, painted,
sculptured, or otherwise made visible.*[15]

One of my all-time favorite hobbies is photography. I love looking through the lens of a camera while I try to capture a story through the image before me. I'm always a bit stunned when I look at the photograph after and realize my camera caught the image a bit differently than what I'd seen with my natural eye. There is more clarity, and the photo reveals the finer details my eye missed. Sometimes, I get frustrated when the intended subject is a little out of focus, and an area I never noticed is now sharp and clear.

After participating in a few photo courses, I discovered an appreciation for the advice offered by the instructor on the pictures I submitted. Each instructor had a great eye for catching details and offered suggestions on how a photo could be improved. They proposed ideas that would enhance my pictures in ways I had never considered.

Years ago, I had the revelation that God wanted to become the Instructor in my life to enhance its image. He knows the areas that are a little out of focus. He pinpoints what I've overlooked (or blatantly ignored) and points out where adjustments need to be made. These days, with so many computer programs like Photoshop, we can easily remove any unattractive details in a photograph. Those five pounds that found me—gone! The wrinkles on my face and the dark circles under my eyes—gone! Every negative aspect of a photo that I don't like can easily be removed with a few clicks of a button.

If only the changes God wanted to see in me were as easy to fix. Unfortunately, changing the actual image everyone sees takes work. If I am serious about losing those five extra pounds, I am going to have to exercise and change my eating habits. The same is true when God takes His lens and brings into focus the areas He wants to adjust in each of our lives. I appreciate how He is gentle as He reveals these areas little by little—don't you, too? It was in His gentle way that He began to zero in on the image I had of myself and show me how my focus was off.

Before I knew Christ, I based my self-worth on everything except Him. This statement from *The Handbook of Bible Application* brought new revelation to me as God used it to change my way of thinking:

> Knowing that we are made in God's image and thus share many of His characteristics provides a solid basis for self-worth. Human worth is not based on possessions, achievements, physical attractiveness, or public acclaim. Instead it is based on being made in God's image. Because we bear God's image, we can feel positive about ourself. Criticizing or downgrading ourself is criticizing what God has made and the abilities He has given us. Knowing that you are a person of worth helps you to love God, know Him personally, and make a valuable contribution to those around you.[16]

As someone who was called to be a stay-at-home mom, I relate well to the importance of finding my self-worth not from *what* I did but from the simple fact that I am made in God's image. I am a person of worth because of who I am in Christ.

One day, I was having a conversation with a friend who had always been a working mom. I'm not sure how Pat's and my decision that I would stay at home with our children became the topic of conversation, but she began to assert her opinion that I was "an anchor around my husband's neck." In her mind, because I did not work outside of the home and contribute financially, I was nothing more than a heavy burden for my husband.

Crushed by her words and her opinion of me, I battled the hurt of that statement for a very long time. Eventually, I found myself wondering who I was. I'd think, "I am a mother, a wife, a daughter, a sister, and a friend," but I didn't really know who Kolleen was. "Who is Kolleen, the person, and what is her purpose?"

After our friend (yes, I still consider her a friend) made the statement about me, I felt very little self-worth. After all, she wasn't the only one with the opinion I wasn't contributing much to the world because I was "just" a stay-at-home mom. (Forget the fact that I was molding the lives of our children!) It took God much convincing—and taking many jobs I knew I shouldn't take—to get me to the place of freedom from opinions. I began to understand that my self-worth is not in what I *do*, but the basis of my self-worth is that I was made in the image of God.

But if the definition of *image* is a physical likeness or representation of someone, how does one represent Christ, whom they have never seen? I began seeking the answer to that question, and the answer, I discovered, was found in my time spent with Him. It's in the Law of Association—the more time we spend time with people, the more we tend to act like them as we pick up their habits and mannerisms—the positive and the negative. Our association with those who have endearing qualities we admire may cause us to consider how we'd like to be more like them.

Over time, the Holy Spirit helped me understand that being made in God's image means that I am a reflection of His character here on earth. As I understood this, I noticed contentment began to fill me, and I felt complete as I found my worth in Him. I became determined to no longer give others the power to make me feel *less than* because I wasn't doing what they thought I should be doing. I became more confident in myself as a person, knowing that God had created me—just as I am—for the purpose of serving Him, not man.

What were we created to do? Reflect God's character to others. One of the first characteristics I learned about God was from reading 1 John 4:16: "And we have known and believed the love that God has for us. *God is love*, and he who abides in love abides in God, and God in him" (emphasis mine). Our reflection of His character should reveal His love. He is love; therefore, we need to also *be* love.

A life lived in Jesus should be bursting with His love for others. God didn't leave us in the dark on how we could sustain His love in our day-to-day interactions; He gifted us with the love chapter in 1 Corinthians 13. The Lord used these verses to teach me and show me His character of love.

> Love is patient, love is kind. It does not envy, it does not boast, it is not proud. It does not dishonor others, it is not self-seeking, it is not easily angered, it keeps no record of wrongs. Love does not delight in evil but rejoices with the truth. It always protects, always trusts, always hopes, always perseveres. (1 Corinthians 13: 4–7 NIV)

Someone offered great advice when they said, "If you want to learn how to live a life of love, put your name where the word love should be." As a young mom trying to learn how to love—I began to do just that. Then I would repeat it over and over. This tactic came in handy when I found myself upset by hurtful words or when I grew impatient with my children; I would speak out: "Kolleen is patient. Kolleen is kind." If I was struggling with jealousy or envy, I would say, "Kolleen does not envy. Kolleen is not proud."

It was life changing. It altered how I viewed myself, and as that changed, I was able to adjust my response to situations I encountered.

I fervently prayed for the Lord to help me to grow and mature in love and in my reflection of His love for others. But we will never reflect His love to others without first accepting it for ourselves. God desires for us to understand this so we can know true contentment. Far too many today strive for success—from the world's perspective—and never find contentment because it's His love for us and our need for Him that we are really looking for. If the body of Christ were to view one another as image-bearers of God, our value and worth would be found in Him alone. Then, we'd become free to admire our similarities and celebrate our differences.

Let's remember, male and female were created equal in *His image*. We no longer need to compete against one another or criticize those with differing opinions. We bear the image of God, and because we were made in His image, we are more than able to reflect Him well.

Changing our identity will, perhaps, warrant a refocus and a reminder that because we bear His image, we must do everything we can to walk in a manner worthy of Him. I want to reflect Him well to those around me, inside the church, as well as outside of it. What about you? Will you lay down your offenses, your critical spirit, and your bitterness toward whoever has offended you and allow others to see God's image through you? It's time to seek God's character in our own lives so we can become a physical representation of Him on earth by seeking to pour out love, patience, forgiveness, kindness, and faithfulness to everyone around us.

Activate, Become, and Confess as you seek to change your identity one letter at a time.

## Activate - Start the Work

- You must know you are a "person of worth" in order to "love God, know Him personally, and make a valuable contribution to those around you." Do you know you are a person of worth? If no, what will you do to see yourself as a person of worth?
- What valuable contribution have you already made because of this knowledge?

## Become – Come into Existence and #beYOU

- Read Colossians 3:1–3. According to these verses, what have you been raised to?
- Because of this, where should your thoughts be focused?
- When do you find it the most difficult to keep your thoughts focused on God's truth?
- How will you refocus your thinking because of knowing your real life is not here on earth?

## Confess – Declare in Faith

I was created in the image of God, and as His image-bearer, I will reflect His character to those around me. Because God is love, I will be love. (Fill your name in the blanks.) _____ is patient and kind. _____ is not jealous or boastful or proud or rude. _____ does not demand her/his own way. _____ is not irritable and keeps no record of being wronged. _____ does not rejoice about injustice but rejoices whenever the truth wins out. _____ never gives up, never loses faith, is always hopeful, and endures through every circumstance (based on 1 Corinthians 13:4–8 NLT).

## Let's pray:

Father God, thank You for the revelation You have given to me that I have been made in Your image. Help me, Father, to carry myself in a manner that represents Your character well. Empower me to leave behind attitudes and opinions that do not align with You. Show me how to think and love just like You do. Enable me to see myself as worthy of Your love and then see others as worthy of it, too. Thank You, Lord, for creating me to be just like You! Amen.

# J Is for *Justified*

God says I am JUSTIFIED.

Therefore let it be known to you, brethren,
that through this Man is preached to you the
forgiveness of sins; and by Him everyone who
believes is *justified* from all things from which
you could not be justified by the law of Moses.
—Acts 13:38–39, emphasis mine

**Justified:** *to declare innocent or
guiltless; absolve; acquit.*[17]

**Absolve:** *to free from guilt or blame
or their consequences.*[18]

I once had a conversation with a friend who believed in God but struggled with the "forgiveness of *any* sin" aspect of Christianity. She, like many of us, believed that people use faith in Christ as an excuse to do whatever they want and then say, "Because I am a Christian, I am forgiven of that." She reasoned that far too many people use the "I am forgiven" card to justify wrong behavior.

One example she shared with me was related to when marriages are broken through infidelity and then the guilty party makes a claim that they've found Christ. Are we to simply believe all is forgiven? After all, families are split up and wounds have been inflicted that some may never recover from.

I can certainly understand her dilemma in this area. It can be hard for any of us to grasp the claim that God can—and will— forgive any and all sin. When we turn on our televisions and hear stories of abuse and scandal, it can be hard to understand how God could possibly forgive the horrific actions committed. She, like so many of us, believed that there must be a price to pay for our choices, and to say that God forgives any wrong action is scandalous. But, God's gift of absolving us from our sin is not about justifying wrong behavior; it is about being justified *from* the wrong behavior.

That is what the Bible is all about. It's the story of redemption. It's the story of a God who loves us and made a way for us to be free from the bondage of our sin. We can read the Bible and see examples of broken people who made mistakes and a God who would reach out in pure love to save them. He brought salvation to us through His one and only Son, Jesus. All who believe in Jesus are justified from all things. He gave His law, but the law couldn't bring forgiveness for sins. Jesus brought that. And when He died, He made it possible for us to become justified before God. Let's take a closer look at that word.

While it is true that there was a sin debt owed to God that I could not pay, Jesus became that payment so I could find forgiveness and eternal life. "For the wages of sin is death, but the free gift of God is eternal life in Christ Jesus our Lord" (Romans 6:23 NLT). I believe that when we refuse to let go of sin, or refuse to believe we are forgiven for our sin, we insult what Jesus did for us on the cross. The Greek word *dikaioō* is translated as *justified*, and it means "to declare, pronounce, one to be just, righteous, or such as he ought to be."[19] Now that is a seed we should take and plant deep into our hearts and allow those words to take root and grow within us.

We are not living *such as we ought to be* when we refuse to believe in the power of God's forgiveness. For what reason did He send His Son if we aren't going to believe that we can be forgiven people?

In our human thinking, we believe we must pay—over and over and over—for our sins. We never want to let anyone off the hook. How many times do people bring up past mistakes in a confrontation with someone, never allowing the person to forget the sins of their past? If we live out of our human nature, that's what we do. But if we live out of our spiritual nature, we understand that God does not do that—and neither should we.

God tells us that when we repent, our sins have been removed from us as far as the east is from the west. Or as The Message Bible says it: "And as far as sunrise is from sunset, he has separated us from our sins" (Psalm 103:12). We must learn to let people off the hook and realize that it is okay to let ourselves off the hook, too. Once we repent with a sincere heart, the sin we commit is under Christ's blood, and we become justified before God. Every time we refuse to let go of our own guilt for a sin, we are telling Jesus His death wasn't enough. I was so convicted by this when the Lord spoke this truth to my heart.

There are times when I allow my mind to take a trip back into history and review all the mistakes of my past. It is funny how that happens. Suddenly a thought sneaks into my mind, and before long, I physically feel the pressing weight of my sins on me. When thoughts of what I've done, the hurts I've caused others, and the shamefulness of it all wash over me, they can become obsessive in my mind. When this happens, fear tries to grip me.

"What if God really does not forgive me? How could He when I cannot even forgive myself?" This thinking pattern leads me right into depression and feelings of rejection. I can become consumed with myself and eat my way through a day. God, in His mercy, gives us new understanding:

> Then I heard a loud voice saying in heaven, "Now salvation, and strength, and the kingdom of our God, and the power of His Christ have come, for the accuser of our brethren, who accused them before our God day and night, has been cast down." (Revelation 12:10)

Satan is the accuser of the brethren—that includes sisters too! He brings the accusations to our minds. When my thoughts turn in the direction of "look at what you've done," or "how could you?" or "how could God forgive you?" it is at that moment that I need to remind myself that God does not accuse—Satan does. God is full of grace, mercy, and conviction. Conviction is when He begins to impress upon me an area that needs attention. Accusations are faultfinding and full of blame that lead to condemnation. Victory over condemnation happens as we learn to recognize the difference between the voice of the accuser and the voice of the Holy Spirit. Memorizing Romans 8:1 can certainly help us fight the battle related to condemning ourselves and others: "There is therefore now no condemnation to those who are in Christ Jesus, who do not walk according to the flesh, but according to the Spirit."

Satan doesn't only bring accusations before God; he also tempts us to bring accusations against one another. That is a good thing to remember when we refuse to let someone off the hook for a failure in his or her life—for example, when I begin to think about how a friend has let me down or how it appears they have failed me. When my mind wanders to a place that brings up accusations against another, I must be quick to recognize the direction my thoughts are taking me. Satan wants to accuse us before God and before one another. If your mind is focused on how horrible the person is or that action was, then you are thinking like the accuser.

Changing your identity is choosing to focus on forgiveness, just as you are forgiven. When we have the faith to believe that God is able to forgive all sins, then we must begin to live like it. We don't dwell on past mistakes. We live like the justified people we are. We don't accuse ourselves or others. God wants us to know that "He who covers his sins will not prosper, but whoever confesses and forsakes them will have mercy" (Proverbs 28:13). The very best way for me to remember that I can stand before God innocent, absolved from, or free from the guilt of all my sins through the sacrifice of Jesus is to remember the definition of *justified* this way: "Just as if I'd never sinned." Now, let's go live like it.

Activate, Become, and Confess as you seek to change your identity one letter at a time.

## Activate - Start the Work

- What is your belief on the forgiveness of God?
- Do you think He does forgive everyone of anything? If not, what situations do you wrestle with?

- How does it feel to know God justifies you—removes your sin and that of others just as if you'd never done it?

## Become – Come into Existence and #beYOU

- Is there anything you rationalize in your life that God calls sin based upon what you know from the Word of God?
- Read 1 John 1:9. What does it say you need to do?
- What does God say He will do? How does that make you feel?
- Write out a sentence that states how you feel about the word *cleanse* when it comes to the condition of your past sin.

## Confess – Declare in Faith

Clearly, God has shown and proven His own love for me because while I was still a sinner, Christ died for me. Therefore, I have been declared free from the guilt of my sin. The blood of Jesus saved me and made it possible for me to be justified. With help from the Holy Spirit, I will no longer make excuses for my sin, but I will cast it out of my life and live just as though I've never sinned (Romans 5:8–10, paraphrased).

## Let's pray:

Father God, thank You for the gift of Jesus, the One who paid the penalty for my sin—the One who saved me from Your wrath because of that sin. Lord, show me where I have been misguided in my thinking regarding forgiveness. If I refuse to let myself off the hook, show me how to do it. When I refuse to let others off the hook, remind me that You have justified them, too. Help me, Lord, to live free from condemnation. We pray in Jesus's mighty name. Amen!

# K Is for *Known*

God says He KNOWS me.

O LORD, You have searched me
and known me.

—Psalm 139:1, emphasis mine

**Know:** *to be acquainted or familiar
with; to perceive directly; have direct
cognition of; to have understanding of.*[20]

O ver the course of more than thirty years of marriage, my husband, Pat, and I have attended six churches. I know that may seem like a lot, especially if you have attended the same church for your entire life. But I believe that God moves you to grow you, and it is important to be flexible and allow Him to place you where He wants you. There may be different reasons why He would move you from one church to another. I recognize now that He moved us out of one church because the teaching was off scripturally. He moved us out of another church, after a time of training, to serve in new one. And then He took us from the place of serving to a place of rest and healing in yet another.

Unfortunately, I can also look back and see a time when we left a church because of a grievance against a new pastor. I'm still not exactly sure why he and I didn't get along, but we didn't. In all honesty though, I will admit now that much of it was due to my immaturity as a Christian. I am not proud of it, but I am not too proud to admit it either. Now, I appreciate that the Lord allowed me to leave a church mad, because He connected me with a pastor who saw the immaturity in me and allowed God to show him that I was worth investing in.

Looking back now, I can say that this was one of the most blessed times and yet, one of the most excruciatingly painful times of my life too. I spent the first two years at our new church crying, as the Lord began to reveal matters of my heart and teach me what death to self really meant. God had taken me—a bulldozer by personality—and put me under the leadership of a pastor who was more like a hand shovel. With my very choleric temperament, it was easy for me to bulldoze my way through each day and over any obstacle in my path. But my pastor was a very patient and gentle teacher, a man who was careful about where and how he chose to turn over the dirt.

I am grateful that he was; I believe he spared me more heart damage because of his compassionate ways. He began the process of digging deep into my heart and helped me uncover the cause of my idiosyncrasies. He helped me understand the importance of allowing someone you trust to dig around in areas that you'd prefer to keep hidden. Secrets are like mold inside of us; if left alone in the dark they will begin to spread and contaminate other areas. Pastor Manny Josbena taught me a valuable life lesson when he helped me understand that my past was to be a place of reference, not a place of residence.

Let that sink in for a moment; our past is a place of reference, not a place of residence.

Living in the past does not allow God the freedom to move us into the future He has planned for us. If you are always looking behind you, how are you able to look forward to your future? A good pastor will be able to help you find healing and wholeness from your broken places.

It was during my time there that God revealed the Beatitudes to me for the first time. One in particular jumped out at me, "Blessed are the pure in heart, For they shall see God" (Matthew 5:8). Because of a pastor who was willing to say hard things to me, I became acquainted with myself, and my heart began to heal from the past. God has always known the person He created me to be. He also knew exactly who I needed in my life to help me discover that person at this point of the journey. I began to grow in my faith, learn how important moving in step with God was, and understand that pure motives flow from a pure heart. God searches us and knows us—authentically— and nothing about us goes unnoticed by Him.

As Jesus traveled through Samaria on His way to Galilee, He met a woman who was alone at Jacob's well. I can imagine the scene: The other women of the community have been to the well, enjoyed the company of friends, gathered their water, and made their way back home by now. This woman, however, has waited until the hottest part of the day, making her way to the well alone. Why does she wait until others were no longer lingering at the well?

Shame isolates you.

We discover—through her conversation with Jesus—that she is a woman who has suffered tremendous loss. This is a woman with scars in her heart. How could she not be? She'd had—and lost—five husbands. Little did she know the morning of that particular day, she would meet a Man who would dig around in her heart and let her know she was worth investing His time in.

When she arrives at the well, Jesus speaks to her, "Give Me a drink" (John 4:7b). It would seem as though there were no pleasantries in their introduction—no, "Hi, I'm Jesus and I'm passing through Samaria on my way to Galilee. What's your name? I don't have anything to draw water with. It's so hot; would you mind giving me a drink? Please?"

When John shared this story, he didn't indicate that type of conversation, but he disclosed the detail that "Jews had no dealings with Samaritans" (vs. 9). Samaritans were considered unclean to a Jew because they were interracial—half Jew and half Gentile.[21] Jews did not invest their time in anyone from Samaria.

I can almost hear the sarcasm roll from her tongue as she responds to Him, "How is it that *You*, being a *Jew*, ask a drink from *me*, a Samaritan woman?" (vs. 9, emphasis mine).

Can you hear it? Or am I the only one whose tongue can deliver sarcasm when hurt within my heart rises to the surface? Is it possible that she has a little edge to her response because she has become cynical as time has gone by? Perhaps it came by way of people who have made her feel as though she were somehow less—by way of the people who knew *about* her, but little *of* her. It's hard to say for sure what her tone is. But remember, she is, after all, at the well alone in the middle of the day. Sometimes our brokenness is exposed through the cynicism in our speech; sometimes it's exposed through our lonely choices. His request for a drink opens the door for this conversation:

> Jesus answered and said to her, "If you knew the gift of God, and who it is who says to you, 'Give Me a drink,' you would have asked Him, and He would have given you living water."
>
> The woman said to Him, "Sir, You have nothing to draw with, and the well is deep. Where then do You get that living water? Are You greater than our father Jacob, who gave us the well, and drank from it himself, as well as his sons and his livestock?"
>
> Jesus answered and said to her, "Whoever drinks of this water will thirst again, but whoever drinks of the water that I shall give him will never thirst. But the water that I shall give him will become in him a fountain of water springing up into everlasting life." (John 4:10-13)

It is here that the woman's ears perk up, "Sir, give me this water, that I may not thirst, nor come here to draw" (vs. 15). In the back of her mind, is she hoping she would never again need to arrange her day around her visit to the well? What is she thirsty for? Acceptance? Freedom? Forgiveness? Understanding?

What does your sin leave you thirsting for?

God knew the woman needed to encounter Jesus that day. When Jesus invested His time and did a little digging into her story, He didn't shy away from talking to her about her lifestyle. She'd been married five times, and while we don't know how those marriages ended, we do know she was living with man number six. He didn't confront the woman with her sin to embarrass her, rather, to help her discover the freedom that comes from repentance and a changed lifestyle. Jesus dug around in the dirt of this woman's heart, and the woman who once avoided the crowd became the woman running to the crowd saying, "Come and see a man who told me everything I ever did. Could he possibly be the Messiah?" (John 4:29 NLT).

That sounds like freedom to me; what about to you? God knows us so well; He knows what we need and the exact moment we need it. Don't fear when He arranges to have someone meet you at the well. He provided me with a pastor who knew how to uncover the damaged soil of my past, releasing me to run into the crowd telling others about Jesus. Shame no longer holds me hostage.

Accepting that God knows us best will change our identity as we rest in the assurance that His plan and purpose for us is to always bring the best for us out of any situation. Psalm 139 helps us to recognize that He knew every one of us before we were born.

> You know my sitting down and my rising up; You understand my thought afar off. You comprehend my path and my lying down, And are acquainted with all my ways. For there is not a word on my tongue, But behold, O Lord, You know it altogether. (Psalm 139:2-4)

God has a plan and intention for your life—every day of it (Psalm 139:16). He is acquainted with all your ways. Ask Him to search you and reveal your heart. Ask Him to show you your anxieties and test you to see if there is any sin in you. Then ask Him to lead you along the path toward everlasting life!

> Your eyes saw my substance, being yet unformed. And in Your book they all were written, The days

fashioned for me, When as yet there were none of them. . . . Search me, O God, and know my heart; Try me, and know my anxieties; And see if there is any wicked way in me, And lead me in the way everlasting. (Psalm 139:16, 23–24)

Activate, Become, and Confess as you seek to change your identity one letter at a time.

## Activate - Start the Work

- God is great at figuring us out when we don't really understand ourselves. Do you allow God to "actively investigate" your heart, or do you shut yourself off from that? What wall is in the way of letting Him have access?
- Do you have an accountability partner you allow to speak into your life? If you don't already have one, who comes to mind as someone who could help you navigate the challenges of life?

## Become – Come into Existence and #beYOU

- It's time to become aware of just how intimately you are *known* by your heavenly Father. Read Psalm 139 and list everything He says about you.

## Confess – Declare in Faith

I will know God and serve Him with a loyal heart and a willing mind. The Lord searches my heart and understands the intent of my every thought. I will seek Him and allow Him to show me He knows me best (inspired by David's instructions to Solomon in 1 Chronicles 28:9).

## *Let's pray:*

Father God, I desire to serve You with a loyal heart and a willing mind; please show me when I step out of line. You are the Searcher of my heart and understand the intent of every thought I have. Show me if I am out of step with Your will. Bring someone into my life that will help me grow spiritually and challenge me to change to be the person You created me to be. I want to be the person You know, not an imposter. In Jesus's name I pray. Amen.

# L Is for *Loved*

## God says I am LOVED.

For I am convinced that neither death nor
life, neither angels nor demons, neither the
present nor the future, nor any powers, neither
height nor depth, nor anything else in all
creation, will be able to separate us from the
*love* of God that is in Christ Jesus our Lord.
—Romans 8:38–39 NIV, emphasis mine

**Love:** *a profoundly tender, passionate
affection for another person; a feeling
of warm personal attachment or
deep affection, as for a parent, child,
or friend.*[22]

I've come to realize that there is one experience that happens in life that I do not really care for. It is the pain of separation. Our children have all grown up, moved out, and now we are separated by distance, and to be honest, I don't like it much. I would love to have them live close enough for us to enjoy Sunday dinners or a visit with the grandkids at my choosing. Our extended families live all over the country, so getting together with the whole family takes an event, like a wedding, or unfortunately, a funeral to pull off.

When I miss my kids, it's easy to mull the *if only* statement over and over in my thinking. *If only* our kids could find closer jobs. *If only* our family could live closer. *If only* I understood why. *If only* we could redo the day we lost our loved one. We have a tendency to live in the *if only*.

The pain of separation is bad enough; but add to it the pain of regret, and it's a heavy burden to carry. That's why I am overcome with immense gratitude when I read the above verse from Romans. Discovering we have the promise that nothing can ever separate us from the love of God was a great comfort to me, and it can be to you, too. Unfortunately for me, there were times that I lived in doubt of that promise. I struggled with the truth of that Scripture because for a long time, I had a belief that I needed to earn God's love. It seemed that whenever I endured the sting of rejection from a close friend, I would wonder how I could trust that God will always love me.

This can become another area in which it is far too easy to live in the *if only*. *If only* I had been a better friend, or *if only* I had a different personality, then we might still be friends. Then, I'd begin to put that same attitude onto God. *If only* I work a little harder or behave a bit better. *If only* I were good enough to earn God's love and acceptance. How blessed and fortunate we are that even though we might want to believe those thoughts, God never said them.

For many years, I was convinced that once I failed God through sin or let Him down through an act of disobedience, I needed to get to work so I could earn His love back. It took a considerable amount of time before I was convinced that I had paid my dues for my sinful act. I assumed that with extra hard work and if I could be good enough, then I might get back in the good graces of God.

Through the years, I have had numerous conversations with women who have expressed the same struggle. We are tricked into believing that only hard work will earn God's love. Could it be because we make others work so hard to get back into our good graces? That's what I finally discovered. I behaved as I believed, and my belief was in a conditional love. If I am a person who does not love unconditionally, I am going to have a hard time believing that God, or anyone, could love me unconditionally. Many days I felt consumed with a love that was full of gush and mush, you know, the feel-good stuff—the love that is all about me. But if I wasn't feeling it on any given day, the love bank was closed. I could pull out my *if only* list and use it to make sure those around me would work hard to meet my needs.

But God never based His love on a "to do" list. His love was never based on my works or my doing everything right. It was simply based on who He is and the fact that He simply loved me—*for me*. Pure and simple, love others because God is Love.

When I read through the Old Testament, I learn so much about the love of God toward a people whose behavior might not have warranted it. While He continued to pour out love, the Israelites continued to pour out complaints, accusations, and rebellion. Yet, because of His unconditional love, instead of turning against them, He continued in His covenant with them. Did He ever become frustrated and angry with them? Yes, He did. He became so angry with them at one point, He wanted to disinherit them. But the Israelites came to discover what Psalm 30:5 reminds us: "His anger lasts only a moment, but his favor lasts a lifetime!" (NLT).

That is the wonderful thing about God. He never shuts off the love valve. It always flows, even in His anger. One of my favorite words of the Bible is the word *nevertheless*, which is found in Psalm 106. This psalm recaps the journey of the Israelites and demonstrates the Lord's mercy. Here we learn that the Israelites rebelled against Him, forgot Him, and tested Him. They envied Moses and Aaron. They worshipped the golden calf and defiled the land. They forgot God was their Savior. The list of their sins is long, and God's wrath was kindled against them, but we see this word come into play—*nevertheless*.

> Nevertheless He saved them for His name's sake, That He might make His mighty power known. . . . Nevertheless He regarded their affliction, When He heard their cry; And for their sake He remembered His covenant, And relented according to the multitude of His mercies. (Psalm 106:8, 44-45)

*Nevertheless* is a sweet reminder that in spite of all that I do, He still says nothing can separate me from His love. Nothing. Oh, there have been times when the Lord seemed distant and I have been tempted to believe that He does not love me—because I have done something that angered Him. But I have heard it said many times that when God seems distant from us, He is not the One who moved. Sin causes separation, not from His love, but from Him.

A Holy God and sin do not mix, and when we sin, we have broken our union with Him. Thankfully, He does not deal with us according to our sins or by what we deserve. In His mercy, like a good parent, He disciplines us. He disciplined the Israelites, and He never stopped loving them. In the same way,

He will never stop loving you or me, even when He needs to discipline us.

There is a huge misconception when it comes to love and discipline. Because we have so little understanding of what real love looks like, we also do not know what loving discipline looks like. Parents are afraid to bring correction or discipline to children nowadays because we fear they will think we do not love them. Or some go to the other extreme and what they call discipline is actually abuse.

It was never easy to discipline our children when they were young. But Pat and I saw early on as new parents that whatever our children thought they could get away with, they were going to try. It was important for our children to understand that discipline came from our love for them. We wanted them to know that boundaries are in place for their protection. If you cross a boundary line that has been put in place to protect you, chances are good that you are going to get hurt.

God has shown me that in the same way, He has boundary lines in place for us. They are a place of protection and safety. When we cross those lines, He is going to get our attention in order to keep us from straying too far. There have been times in my own life when God would bring someone to speak a word of warning to me because I was in disobedience. Sometimes I would heed the warning, but other times I just got mad and refused to listen. I had a very hard time listening to what I did not want to hear. Proverbs 19:20 is an important verse to remember, "Listen to advice and accept discipline, and at the end you will be counted among the wise" (NIV).

God's love runs deep for us and He will send a warning when necessary. We must be careful that we pay attention to them. None of us is immune from His discipline. We need to find security in knowing "that as a man disciplines his son, so the Lord your God disciplines you" (Deuteronomy 8:5

91

NIV). Discipline is never fun to endure but we can learn from Hebrews 12:

> No discipline seems pleasant at the time, but painful. Later on, however, it produces a harvest of righteousness and peace for those who have been trained by it. (Hebrews 12:11 NIV)

I may still say "if only" every now and then when it comes to wanting my family to live closer. But, changing my identity involves relinquishing the belief that *if only* applies to my need to work harder, or do better, to earn the Lord's love. The same is true for you! Instead, we can allow the word *nevertheless* to flow from our lips when we've flubbed things up and the devil would want us to focus on a failure. If God can say it, then we can, too. *Nevertheless* is a much better word; don't you agree?

Activate, Become, and Confess as you seek to change your identity one letter at a time.

## Activate - Start the Work

- How have you mistakenly tied your identity to your works (what you do)?
- In what ways do you sometimes try to earn love?
- Read Psalm 106:7-8. What did the Israelites do? How did God respond?
- Read James 2:14-26. What do you learn from these verses about faith and works and how they work together?

## Become – Come into Existence and #beYOU

- Read 1 John 4:7-9. How do these verses describe God?
- How do they describe you, as a child of God?

- What encouragement from this passage can you apply to your own struggle with wanting acceptance and love?

## Confess – Declare in Faith

I'm absolutely convinced that nothing—nothing living or dead, angelic or demonic, today or tomorrow, high or low, thinkable or unthinkable—absolutely nothing can get between me and God's *love* because of the way that Jesus our Master has embraced me (Romans 8:38–39, paraphrased from NIV).

## *Let's pray:*

Father, forgive me when I fail to remember the abundance of Your mercy and grace and allow rebelliousness to rise up within me. I am grateful that I will never need to wonder if I am loved by You. You never withhold love; You will be faithful to walk with me through my missteps and offer me nevertheless moments. Thank You for Your heart of love for me; You can't help but love me—it's Who You are! Amen.

# M Is for *Mind*

God says I have the MIND of Christ.

"For who has known the mind of the LORD
that he may instruct Him?"
But we have the *mind* of Christ.
—1 Corinthians 2:16, emphasis mine

**Mind:** *intellect or understanding, as
distinguished from the faculties of
feeling and willing; intelligence.*[23]

You have probably read at least one children's book written by Dr. Seuss, at one time or another. I enjoyed reading them to my children as well as the little ones in my life these days. These are wonderful stories full of rhyme that really give me a good chuckle at times! He wrote so many great ones that it's hard to pick a favorite, but one I really love is *Oh the Thinks You Can Think*. It's a wonderful tale that encourages children to, you guessed it, think!

"You can think about red. You can think about pink. You can think up a horse. Oh, the thinks you can think! Oh the thinks you can think up if only you try. . . . Think left and think right and think low and think high, oh the thinks you can think up if only you try!"[24]

It sure is a cute book for children, and we love to encourage children to "use their imagination," don't we? I love watching children use their imagination. However, as adults, sometimes the things that we "think up if only we try" may not be exactly the "thinks" that we should be thinking. Sometimes the private conversation I have inside my head is a conversation that I know should not be taking place. And while no one around me knows what I'm thinking, God always does. And He has a way of letting me know when my thoughts are not pleasing to Him. We have been given a warning as to what we should do with those types of conversations when we are told to bring "every thought into captivity to the obedience of Christ" (2 Corinthians 10:5).

The Amplified Bible puts it like this: "We are destroying sophisticated arguments and every exalted and proud thing that sets itself up against the [true] knowledge of God, and we are taking every thought and purpose captive to the obedience of Christ." As a child, we use our imagination for entertainment purposes, but as an adult, we must take control of our mind and not allow our imagination to run wild. Our mind can become a dangerous tool if we aren't careful.

I'm confident that I am not the only person who has allowed my imagination to get the best of me. I can imagine all sorts of things! There have been times when someone has walked by me and did not say hello or (supposedly) gave me a funny look, and my initial assumption is that I must have done something to make them mad. After our brother-in-law was killed in a car accident, if my husband was five minutes late pulling into the driveway from work, I stood at the window, imagining the same tragedy happening to him. A physical symptom can make me imagine a deadly illness in a few days' time. A small argument with my husband can lead to imagining a marriage crisis, ending with divorce and a division of property!

I have a really good imagination, and if I don't guard my mind, I can conceive all sorts of negativity. Every single thought that I allow to have access to my mind, if I am not careful, can easily become a consuming one. Eventually, they can become crippling thoughts that will prevent me from living how God intended for me to live. That is why Paul told us to cast "down imaginations" and bring "every thought into captivity to the obedience of Christ" (MEV). In the Greek, the word *casting* is *kathaireō*, which means "to throw down, with the use of force."[25]

When the thoughts in our mind are not consistent with the Word, we need to throw them out—by force if necessary. Isn't that a powerful thought? We are to become forceful in our thinking when our mind is being used for anything other than how God intended. We take our thoughts captive, and it needs to be done on a regular basis. The moment our mind begins to drift in the wrong direction, we have to take action to protect it.

Throughout history, there have been many wars fought and many prisoners of war taken. When someone is taken captive do you think the abductor does so by simply asking nicely, "Excuse me, would you please come with me? I am taking you captive now."

Absolutely not.

When you capture something, it is usually done in a forceful manner. That is exactly how we must protect our minds against the Enemy who desires to take our thoughts captive by turning our focus to the wrong thing. God's enemy is our enemy, and Satan knows that if we actually begin to think like Christ, we will be powerful for God's kingdom. My goodness! Can you imagine how your life could change if only you thought like Christ? But we must be the ones to take every thought captive so all our thoughts are obedient to Christ. Not just some: all.

That means making sure our minds are surrendered to Christ alone. We cannot afford to allow every thought that enters to just come in and make itself comfortable on the park bench of our minds.

You know how that goes, right? The thought is planted, and we mull it over and over again. We allow it to fester and before we know it, it is all we think about. When we do that, depression sets in, friendships die, unfaithfulness enters a marriage, suicide ends a life, churches become apathetic, and bitterness over our disappointment begins to rule our heart.

If we are going to "cast down imaginations," then it means learning to discern between two things—our imagination and God's truth. Imagination is defined as "the faculty of imagining, or of forming mental images or concepts of what is not actually present to the senses."[26] In Greek, the word for *imagination* is *logismos*, and it is defined as "a reckoning; reasoning: such as is hostile to the Christian faith; a judgment or decision."[27]

How do we know when our thoughts are "hostile to the Christian faith"? By knowing the truth about the Christian faith. We must know the Word of God. If we don't know what the Word says or we take the Word out of the context of its actual meaning, we will not be able to discern between truth and error. We are told in 1 Corinthians 2:14 that "the natural man does not receive the things of the Spirit of God, for they are foolishness to him; nor can he know them, because they are spiritually discerned." The natural man—the unspiritual side of our human nature—is who we are before we have accepted Christ as our Savior, and he does not have the Spirit of God living inside of him. When a Christian states a truth from the Word of God, the natural man thinks it is foolish. We sure can see that in our culture today, can't we?

There have been times over the years when I've had to fight for my mind because of natural "men." The more I learn about God and the more I understand about His ways, the less the natural man—a person who is not filled with the Spirit—can understand me. At times, this can be very difficult when family and friends do not understand the changes in your life. People may not understand why you will no longer do the things you would have done with them in the past. The stand you take for God now will make no sense to those who do not know Christ. It seems like foolishness to them.

Every minute of every day we are presented with three different opportunities for where we can allow our mind to wander. We can choose to allow it to wander to the places that are pleasing to God, to the places Satan directs, or to the places that please others. We must make the right choice—every time—if we are going to be successful in "casting down arguments and every high thing that exalts itself against the knowledge of God, and bringing every thought into captivity to the obedience of Christ" (2 Corinthians 10:5).

When we allow God to have control of our mind, our thoughts become filled with the desire to glorify, serve, and consider Him, as we endeavor to respect His ways and His word.

When our mind is on God, it is on His Word and on truths that allow us to grow and mature in our faith in Him. There is peace within me when my mind is focused on Him. There is a promise for us in Isaiah 26:3 which says; "You will keep him in perfect peace, Whose mind is stayed on You, Because he trusts in You."

The more of the Word I get into me, the more of the Word I focus on, the more peaceful my life is. When I allow the circumstances of life and the trials of life to take control of my thoughts, I can easily become a wreck. I get all flustered and irritated, and anxiety rises within me. When a situation could consume my mind, I must first be willing to recognize what I am focused on. When the Lord shows me my focus is on the wrong thing, I need to quickly speak the truth of God's Word over that situation.

The Word tells us that we "have the mind of Christ" (2 Corinthians 2:16), but as Christians, we must *desire* to have the mind of Christ more than anything else. Romans 11:34 tells us that no one can comprehend all the ways of God. But through the guidance of the Holy Spirit who is living in me, I can have spiritual insight into God's plans, His actions, and His ways of thinking. So how do we get the mind of Christ? Only through knowing the Word of God.

As we study the Word and get it into our hearts, next we begin to make the Word of God our confession. Speak the truth of God's Word out of your mouth and you will see the thoughts of your mind change. We can confess God's promises over the situations we go through in life. He wants our speech to be about Him and all He has done, is doing, and will do in the future. We could not, and would not, do that if our mind were focused on all our woes and troubles. If we wonder how to go about getting our minds set on things above, a good place to start is found in Philippians.

Summing it all up, friends, I'd say you'll do best by filling your minds and meditating on things true, noble, reputable, authentic, compelling, gracious—the best, not the worst; the beautiful, not the ugly; things to praise, not things to curse. Put into practice what you learned from me, what you heard and saw and realized. Do that, and God, who makes everything work together, will work you into his most excellent harmonies. (Philippians 4:8 MSG)

Our identity will change when we begin to look for God in all situations and make *Him* the talk of the town! The abundant life can be ours when our minds are set on all things worthwhile and worthy of praise. Don't you agree?

Activate, Become, and Confess as you seek to change your identity one letter at a time.

## Activate - Start the Work

- How active is your imagination when it comes to relationships with others?
- How well do you protect your thoughts from enemy attacks?
- Make a list of thoughts you find yourself consistently tripping over and then discard the list. Then write out Philippians 4:8 as a replacement for those thoughts.

## Become – Come into Existence and #beYOU

- To have the *mind* of Christ, we need to spend time with Him. How much time to you devote to the study of His Word?
- Where could you make changes to allow for more time to know His Word?

## Confess – Declare in Faith

Because I have the mind of Christ, I am able to think thoughts that are true, pure, right, holy, friendly, and proper. I will cast down every thought that does not line up with the Word of God. I will not allow my mind to be a storehouse for the Enemy's lies.

### Let's pray:

Lord, I want Your thoughts to be my thoughts. I want to think like You do in every situation I face. When I allow my mind to wander down a path that will take me to a dangerous place, please pull me back quickly. Help me to recognize right away when my mind has become a target of the Enemy. Give me the courage to say no to any thought that does not please or glorify You. In Jesus's name, I pray. Amen.

# N Is for *New*

God says I am a NEW creation.

Therefore, if anyone is in Christ, he is a *new*
creation; old things have passed away; behold,
all things have become *new.*
—2 Corinthians 5:17, emphasis mine

**New:** *of a kind now existing or
appearing for the first time; fresh or
unused; other than the former.*[28]

As I have been studying and contemplating this word, *new,* the Lord has drawn me to two very different creatures. Caterpillars and the apostle Paul—one, an insect that transforms into a beautiful butterfly, and the other, a strict Pharisee who God transformed into an apostle; a man fully surrendered to Jesus Christ.

I am awestruck by the radical changes that happened in the life of Paul. Just as a caterpillar sheds his skin (several times) and comes out of his cocoon a completely different being, Paul shed his Pharisee skin, went into the cocoon of separation from his old life, and became a completely different being. I have loved getting to know Paul. Let's look at his story.

Saul (Paul was his Greek name) was born in Tarsus the son of a Pharisee from the tribe of Benjamin, and he was raised in the strictest of Jewish homes. We learn in Acts 23:6 that he considered himself "a Pharisee, the son of a Pharisee." He studied with Gamaliel, one of the leading Pharisaic teachers of the time. He was greatly respected. In Acts 22:3 Paul said, "I am indeed a Jew, born in Tarsus of Cilicia, but brought up in this city at the feet of Gamaliel, taught according to the strictness of our fathers' law, and was zealous toward God as you all are today."

Paul was a student of the law and he loved it, and because of this, he was determined to keep the law—at any cost. With his own words, he said: "You know what I was like when I followed the Jewish religion—how I violently persecuted God's church. I did my best to destroy it. I was far ahead of my fellow Jews in my zeal for the traditions of my ancestors" (Galatians 1:13–14 NLT).

Have you ever been so set in your ways that you could not see beyond it? When there was no other way than your own? I know I have, and I believe this to be exactly how Saul viewed the Jewish law. It was the only way. Which is why Saul was so determined to see the Christian movement stopped. In his mind, it just wasn't the right way. Paul goes on to say, "I persecuted the followers of this Way to their death, arresting both men and women and throwing them into prison, as the high priest and all the Council can themselves testify. I even obtained letters from them to their associates in Damascus, and went there to bring these people as prisoners to Jerusalem to be punished" (Acts 22:4–5 NIV).

It's easy to see Saul's passion for his faith in the law of God, isn't it? He was raised in the law, he knew the law, and he was determined that all were going to follow that law. Saul was radical in his law-abiding ways, and for the Lord to reach him, He was going to have to reveal Himself in a radical sort of way. That is exactly what He did. Acts 9 tells the details of Paul's conversion on the road to Damascus.

> Meanwhile, Saul was still breathing out murderous threats against the Lord's disciples. He went to the high priest and asked him for letters to the synagogues in Damascus, so that if he found any there who belonged to the Way, whether men or women, he might take them as prisoners to Jerusalem. As he neared Damascus on his journey, suddenly a light from heaven flashed around him. He fell to the ground and heard a voice say to him, "Saul, Saul, why do you persecute me?"
>
> "Who are you, Lord?" Saul asked.
>
> "I am Jesus, whom you are persecuting," he replied. "Now get up and go into the city, and you will be told what you must do."
>
> The men traveling with Saul stood there speechless; they heard the sound but did not see anyone. Saul got up from the ground, but when he opened his eyes he could see nothing. So they led him by the hand into Damascus. For three days he was blind, and did not eat or drink anything. (Acts 9:1–9 NIV)

Three days blind and waiting; can you imagine the thoughts he had to work through in his mind during those three days? I imagine the scene played over and over in his mind as he told anyone that would listen, "I was just walking along the road when suddenly. . ."

And while he sat waiting, another man, Ananias, was receiving his instructions to go to Saul and lay hands on him to heal him (Acts 9:10–16). Despite Ananias's hesitations, he knew God had called this man to the work of the Christian faith—the way of Jesus. I love the declaration God made to Ananias about who Saul was to Him. Saul was His chosen instrument to carry His name to the Gentiles (vs. 15).

God had a plan and purpose for Saul his entire life. Nothing of his life would be wasted, in the same way God will use everything in your life for His glory, too. Something like scales fell from Saul's eyes and just like that, he could see again. Only this time, he saw truth. He saw Jesus for who Jesus really was—the Son of God and the one true Way. He saw his life with a new purpose, a new call, and a new passion. He wasted absolutely no time as the Word goes on to say, "At once he began to preach in the synagogues that Jesus is the Son of God" (Acts 9:20).

What an incredible example of old things passing away and all things becoming new. He became a new man. He changed from Saul the defender of the law to Saul the defender of Jesus. He would begin using his Greek name, Paul, as his mission in life changed when he accepted the call of God to be an apostle to the Gentiles.

Now you may be wondering what Paul (Saul) and caterpillars have in common. The answer is: transformation. The process a caterpillar must go through to become something entirely different is one often used to describe what happens when God removes scales from unseeing eyes. And wow, I can relate to that! Like Paul, I had to have scales removed from my eyes so I could see the real Jesus, not the one I had imagined Him to be, desired for Him to be, or even professed Him to be. A caterpillar sheds its old skin as it grows and develops, and like Saul had to shed his old skin of a Pharisee, I also needed to shed old skin as I became His new creation.

Shedding old patterns of thinking, bad habits, and rotten attitudes isn't necessarily a fun process, but it's a crucial one. It's one I often have a difficult time embracing and have a tendency to give some pushback to. It's easy to make excuses for why you shouldn't need to change, but imagine what would happen to the caterpillar that argued about going into the cocoon. It would die, never fully developing into the beauty God always intended.

I think that's why God needed to blind Saul to get him to where He wanted him. He was so sure he was right; he was sincere—but sincerely wrong—and his misguided passion led him to do some very unloving and ungodly things. So, while Saul was relentless in his determination to carry out his plan, God used blindness to move him into his cocoon where He could begin the transformation process.

From the inside of a cocoon no one can see the miraculous things taking place. The same is true for the changes God makes within the privacy of each heart that is willing to surrender fully to Him. Paul told the Romans that they were not to "copy the behavior and customs of this world;" instead, they were to "let God transform you into a new person by changing the way you think" (Romans 12:2a NLT). I hear experience talking. He tells us that this is how we "will learn to know God's will for you, which is good and pleasing and perfect" (12:2b NLT). Amazing changes occur in us when we hold nothing back from God and we learn to submit to His plan and will.

When Saul's sight was restored, he got up and never went back to his old way of life. The butterfly never again returns to the life of a caterpillar; it remains a butterfly. That's where many of us lose out. We might have a great conversion experience and be ready to go with God but then be stopped by fear when God begins to ask us to shed some old skin. We might also believe our past disqualifies us from the future God has planned for us. But, Paul never allowed his past to disqualify him; he used it as part of his testimony for God. He wasn't afraid to admit to the actions of the man he once was because he knew he was no longer that person. He was determined to have everyone understand the old life was full of corruption and decay, but a new life in Christ was full of righteousness and holiness (Ephesians 4:22-24).

Every now and then, I might find myself slipping back into one of those old bad habits, and when I do, I know I have a choice to make: surrender to the habit or get closer to God. If I truly want to change into the one God has intended, the choice is easy.

Changing our identity to become the new creation God intended will require our allowing Him to do the new thing. How can we live in the new life if we fear letting go of the old one? We also need to allow one another to change, and we need to encourage one another as we learn to walk in our new identity. Change can be very hard, and we need one another to help support us during those times. God has so much in store for each one of us in the new life He has planned for us. I have no doubt we are capable of living there.

Activate, Become, and Confess as you seek to change your identity one letter at a time.

### Activate - Start the Work

- Sometimes change can seem overwhelming. Where does Psalm 61:2 tell us to go when we are overwhelmed?

- When have you sought God as your safe refuge? How did it feel to be in that place?

## Become – Come into Existence and #beYOU

- Paul's mission in life changed following his incredible encounter with Jesus. How has your purpose in life changed because of yours?

### Confess – Declare in Faith

I confess that I am a new creation in Christ! The day I accepted Jesus, the old me was gone and I was made *new*. God has permission to develop love, joy, peace, patience, kindness, goodness, faithfulness, gentleness, and self-control within me so I can be free to be me! The new me.

## *Let's Pray:*

Father, I ask You to reveal any area within me that You recognize to be unholy and unrighteous. When deception has blinded me to You, Lord, You have permission to wrap me up in a "cocoon" to reveal Your truth to me. My heart's desire is to be the new creation for which You sent Jesus to the cross in order for me to become. I don't want to do the same thing I've always done and yet expect something different in my life. I want to step out from under the heavy burden of the past and into a new life with You. We pray in Jesus's name. Amen.

# O Is for *Overcome*

God says I have OVERCOME.

"And they *overcame* him by the blood of the
Lamb and by the word of their testimony, and
they did not love their lives to the death."
—Revelation 12:11, emphasis mine

**Overcome:** *to get the better of in a
struggle or conflict; conquer; defeat; to
prevail over.*[29]

W e've worked through the letter M, where we learned we have the *mind* of Christ, and the letter N, where we learned we are *new* in Christ. Next, I believe we need to talk about *overcoming*—letter O—the battles that would keep us locked in our old ways of thinking and living. The word *overcome* in the original Greek is *nikaō*, which means "to conquer." This definition includes: "to carry off the victory, come off victorious."

The victories include those "of Christ, victorious over all His foes; of Christians, that hold fast their faith even unto death against the power of their foes, and temptations and persecutions; when one is arraigned or goes to law, to win the case, maintain one's cause."[30]

Jesus had a very important message to share with his disciples when He said this:

> I have told you these things, so that in Me you may have [perfect] peace. In the world you have tribulation and distress and suffering; but be courageous [be confident, be undaunted, be filled with joy]; I have overcome the world." [My conquest is accomplished, My victory abiding.] (John 16:33 AMP)

Let's just wrap ourselves in that promise we have from Jesus, Himself. He overcame the world so we could too. We can learn so much from Jesus through His teachings in the Word. And one area He wants us to be aware of is our authority over the Enemy of our souls—Satan himself.

As Christians, we must be aware that we have a very real enemy—one who is out to deceive us and keep as many people away from God as he can. He is a thief, a liar, and a destroyer. Jesus explained the thief's purpose was to steal, kill, and destroy (John 10:10a). This is the total opposite of why Christ said He came: "I have come that they may have life, and that they may have it more abundantly" (John 10:10b). Satan's desire is to keep Christians from the abundant life Christ died to give us. He will use whatever tactics he can to get us off the path God has for us. His intent is for us to believe we cannot overcome our struggles. He yearns for us to settle into a life far less than God intends for us to live. He delights when we believe that we are better off doing things our way than God's way.

Our most powerful tool against the Enemy is faith, and he wants to strip us of it. My pastor once said that the only thing we bring to the house of the Lord is faith. "We walk by faith, not by sight" (2 Corinthians 5:7). Smith Wigglesworth said, "I am not moved by what I see. I am moved only by what I believe. I know this—no man looks at appearances if he believes. No man considers how he feels if he believes. The man who believes God has it."[31]

What moves you? In order to overcome the Enemy's schemes and put an end to his plans to steal, kill, and destroy us, we must not be moved by him but instead hold fast to our confession of faith.

Picture in your mind, if you will, a huge mountain that stands before you and you must get to the top of it. You have no choice but to climb this mountain. It's mandatory for everyone. On the side of that mountain are two paths—one very wide, and the other very narrow.

Each path looks as though it will take you to the top of that mountain. The difference is the very narrow path is high above the other and will require great effort on your part. If you take this path, you will have to walk carefully, watching closely every step you take.

The lower path, however, is very wide, looks comfortable to walk on, and the view doesn't look bad either. Remember, it's necessary that you climb that mountain, so you must decide to take the upper or lower path.

The paths begin at the same place; all you must do is walk through a gate and decide which path to take—the wide one or the narrow one.

At the gate to the upper path is a guide to help those who choose to walk it. He has a map for each person that explains the entire climb and shows the path you must take to reach the top safely. It prepares you for every trial you will face along the way. It reveals traps set by enemies and will be a helpful tool for your safety as you walk along the narrow path. The only thing you must do to ensure your safety along this path is to follow the guide's instructions completely. He knows the path. He knows the way to the top of the mountain. He will get you to the top, but only if you carefully walk the direction he tells you to walk and follow his commands, otherwise you risk falling off the path and causing injury to yourself.

As those who walk on the upper narrow path begin their journey, they discover that they have a lot to overcome to get up to this path. This mountain is steep, and to reach the upper path there is a hard climb involved. Many have brought excessive baggage with them that they thought they might need along the way. They soon learn that they are going to have to let it go if they want to reach that narrow path. The climb is too steep to try to hold unnecessary items. The guide knows what you will need and what you will not need, so you can trust him and let go of what he tells you to. Some decide it's too hard to let go of the items that they've brought along, so they turn and decide to walk back to the wider path.

The guide at the gate to the lower path does not have a map for you but assures you that this path is the better choice of the two. Less work. Less struggle. You can do things your way and in your time on this path, just like a nice stroll in the park. You watch for a moment as those around you make their choices. You notice that there are many people who choose to walk on the lower, wide path and they seem to know what they are doing. The guide assures you that the view from this path is the one you want to see.

You weigh your options and decide to take the lower path while others make the decision to walk on the upper path. You begin your journey, but soon you discover that this path does not look quite like you thought it did from the gate. As you walk around the side, the path dips down very low and becomes covered in fog. There are many roots from the trees in the path, and it is not maintained very well.

As you trip over things, stumble, and fall, you realize that this path is so difficult to walk on. Yet in the beginning, it seemed to be the easiest route. Because of the dense fog, it is hard to see, so you stick close to those walking with you; every next step you take is a guessing game. The view that looked so pretty at the gate has quickly become murky and gray. Hope soon turns to hopelessness as you feel your way along this path.

Fear sets in, as there seems to be no way off this path or out of this situation. Along the way you pick up baggage that others from the upper path have dropped, thinking you might need to hold on to that to use later.

You believed there would be less pain involved if you took the lower path because it did not seem as difficult as the upper path. But now, the guide that you thought was there to help you along this path has shown his true colors. He is a deceiver. He has left everyone to fend for themselves. He delights in watching everyone struggle along the path. You discover he is no help at all. His only desire is to watch everyone stumble and fall, as they become frustrated, angry, confused, insecure, and disheartened. His true intention was to keep everyone from the upper path and that "other" guide.

He really hates that other guide. So he just tries to keep people from going to the upper path. Every so often there is a path that leads to the upper one, but he fights any attempt someone makes to leave his path. He loves to watch lost people fail in their attempts to find their way off the lower path. Through trickery and deception, he will make them think there is no way out.

> You can enter God's Kingdom only through the narrow gate. The highway to hell is broad, and its gate is wide for the many who choose that way. But the gateway to life is very narrow and the road is difficult, and only a few ever find it. (Matthew 7: 13–14 NLT)

Satan is hoping we never find that narrow path. If we begin to walk on it, he hopes we will grow weary of it and get off. If he can convince us to not walk the higher path, then he can kick his heels in celebration. Satan is the accuser who stands before God and accuses us night and day (Revelation 12:10). Every time you or I slip up, he's right there to point it out to the Father. That's why we need Jesus Christ who is the Guide to the upper path. The blood Jesus shed covered all of our sins, and when Satan accuses us, Jesus stands up and says, "That sin has been covered by My blood, Father."

This is one way we overcome Satan, according to Revelation 12:11—by the blood of the Lamb. Jesus's blood became the atoning sacrifice—the one that bought our freedom—to overcome our sin debt that we couldn't pay.

The verse in Revelation 12 goes on to say that we also overcome Satan by the Word of our testimony. The Word is *logos*, the spoken Word of God. We overcome Satan by speaking the Word of God as a testimony to what we've seen God do in our lives. As Christians, we can choose to allow the world and all its suffering to overcome us, or we can overcome the world by the power of the Word. If we want to be overcome *by* the world, then we speak negative, hopeless, fearful statements. We can voice our problems continuously and focus solely on them. Or we can change our identity and *overcome* the world, along with the trials and tribulations that we face in the world, by committing to the path God wants us on.

Go to His Word to find your promises, and then give testimony to them. Speak the Word of God over the situation. How can we know what the truth is when we are in the middle of a situation? Scripture is always the safest place to go when searching for truth. It is the only Word of Truth and the only way we overcome. The Word of God shows us the way to the narrow path of blessing. The Message Bible puts Psalm 119:1 this way:

> You're blessed when you stay on course, walking steadily on the road revealed by GOD. You're blessed when you follow his directions, doing your best to find him. That's right—you don't go off on your own; you walk straight along the road he set.

Activate, Become, and Confess as you seek to change your identity one letter at a time.

## Activate - Start the Work

- It's important to understand your enemy. List your understanding of Satan, his minions, and their ways.
- Then read Isaiah 14:12–21 and explain what you think took place in this passage.
- In what ways has the Enemy tried to get you to take a wrong path?

## Become – Come into Existence and #beYOU

- Read Matthew 4. How did Jesus overcome Satan?

- What is your plan for how will you *overcome* Satan the next time he tries to direct you to the wrong path?
- Read Psalm 119:101–105. What promise does God's Word offer to you?
- What does it look like in your life for you to refuse to walk on the path of evil?

## Confess – Declare in Faith

God resists the proud but gives grace to the humble. Therefore, I will humble myself under His mighty hand. I know God cares for me, so I will give my burdens to Him so the Enemy cannot use my burdens to trip me. The Enemy is my adversary, and he seeks to devour me, but I can resist him because of the blood of Jesus Christ. I will overcome him with my testimony and God's Word (inspired by 1 Peter 5:5–8).

## Let's Pray:

Lord Jesus, thank You for offering Your blood—Your life—as the sacrifice that would enable me to overcome the Enemy. Give me insight about his schemes that would keep me bound to sin. Don't let me be deceived by his lies and reveal his true self when he masquerades as an angel of light (2 Corinthians 11:14). I worship You, and You alone, Lord Jesus. Remind me often that I can overcome the devil because he is already a defeated foe. Amen.

# P Is for *Purpose*

God says He has a PURPOSE for my life.

The LORD will fulfill His *purpose* for me;
Your mercy, O LORD, endures forever; do not
forsake the works of Your hands.
—Psalm 138:8 MEV, emphasis mine

**Purpose:** *the reason for which
something exists or is done, made,
used, etc.*[32]

I am a planner. I like to have a strategy for everything. And because I am a planner, I have a family of planners. Our need to organize all the details used to drive our daughter-in-law a bit crazy (that is, until she saw the value of it!). In September, I want to know what we are doing for Thanksgiving. In October, Christmas plans need to be ironed out. I work best with a blueprint in mind. So, you might think that having eighteen years to prepare for the day we would become empty nesters would be enough time for me. But when our youngest son graduated from high school, and I stepped into a new season of life, I became a little distressed. I didn't have a plan ready and waiting for me!

Throughout the years, while I was at home doing the "mommy" job, I had some ideas of what I *thought* I would be doing as this day approached, but when the day finally arrived, not one of those dreams had become a reality. Let me tell you, I had some pretty grandiose ambitions for myself. So, when I became an empty nester without any of my plans being fulfilled, I can honestly say I was not prepared for the extent of emotion that I had to work through. I began to wonder where I fit. I began to lose sight of having any purpose or any direction. Asking the Lord to reveal my purpose was forefront in my heart. I *needed* to know He had a use for me. That He hadn't forgotten about me.

Because frankly, I thought He had forgotten.

I assumed my dreams and desires were the same as God's and they'd fall into place perfectly when the time came. But it seemed every attempt to fulfill a dream led to a crushing failure. So eventually, I settled into a holding pattern (and not a particularly joyful one). While waiting, I began to study, and I began to seek. Then I began to discover, and I began to change.

One discovery I made was the need I had to *be* someone. I wanted my life to mean something. I desperately wanted to know that my life had purpose. And now, as I have traveled along this journey, I recognize this is a longing deep inside each of us. I know you long for purpose, too. And while we want our lives to matter, we will search and search until we discover that our real reason for existing is for God. We were created by Him, for Him, to bring Him glory.

> For in him all things were created: things in heaven and on earth, visible and invisible, whether thrones or powers or rulers or authorities; all things have been created through him and for him. (Colossians 1:16 NIV)

Pastor Rick Warren wrote a devotional book called *The Purpose Driven Life.* If you want to read a book that inspires you to find your true purpose in Christ, this is a good one. He begins the very first chapter with this statement:

> It's not about you. The purpose of your life is far greater than your own personal fulfillment, your peace of mind, or even your happiness. It's far greater than your family, your career, or even your wildest dreams and ambitions. If you want to know why you were placed on this planet, you must begin with God. You were born *by* his purpose and *for* his purpose.[33]

What a transforming revelation it was when it finally clicked inside my heart that God made me for Him, and He knows the plan and purpose He has for my life! I'd always sought ways to find fulfillment and purpose for myself in an effort to make me happy. I gained freedom when He made me aware that He did, indeed, have a plan for my life, and a big part of that was to make sure everything I do is for His glory. He spoke through the prophet Jeremiah, "For I know the plans I have for you . . . plans to prosper you and not to harm you, plans to give you hope and a future" (Jeremiah 29:11 NIV). When I see how he had plans for his children of Israel—even in the midst of their rebellion—I take comfort in knowing he has plans for me too. His plan for each of us is full of hope and prosperity. But there are days when we might find it difficult to hold on to that statement.

Throughout our lifetime we will have experiences that are great, and some not so great. In fact, some might be so devastating that it may seem difficult to even function. But God is faithful—so faithful that He promises to use every painful experience we go through for His glory. Yes, this includes the occasions that cause the most damage to our heart and every event we can't possibly comprehend ever coming out from under. He knows that He can bring something good out of everything. We just need to let Him do it. This is His promise:

> And we know [with great confidence] that God [who is deeply concerned about us] causes all things to work together [as a plan] for good for those who love God, to those who are called according to His plan and purpose. (Romans 8:28 AMP)

Notice that this verse is about allowing ourselves to rely on the knowledge that He can work all things together for good as they fit into a plan. We may not always know what the plan is right away, but God is always a good God, working on our behalf to bring the good and display His glory. He can be trusted to help us in our times of need.

A few months after our son graduated and moved out of the house, one of our best friends was killed in an automobile accident. It was as though the earth stopped turning for us. We had planned and dreamed about the future and what God was going to do with our lives together. And then one day we got a phone call that his life on earth was gone. Once again, I felt as though I was struggling to understand my purpose and my place and what good could come from such a tragic loss. But I asked the Lord over and over, "Show me where I can find You in this situation, Lord. It hurts, and I am full of pain and sorrow, but I want to see Your glory in it." I had to trust His plan rather than my own reasoning and limited understanding.

If we'd concede that we are created by God and for God, then we'd recognize that we cannot trust in ourselves—or in our own abilities—to obtain purpose. True contentment with our purpose will only be found in a life surrendered to Christ. When we allow ourselves to believe our purpose depends solely on our abilities and accomplishments, we run the risk of suffering great disappointment.

We all experience tragedy from time to time. We contemplate what we should be doing, now that we have our college degree. Or like I did, we wonder what we should do, now that the kids have all moved out of the house. If we are not careful, selfishness and pride can very easily become the driving force behind our desire to find purpose. If I leave God out—and I allow my focus to be on me and on what I feel my purpose is in life or what I want my purpose to be—I can very easily become self-centered and self-serving.

But what happens if I do not fulfill the purpose I believe I am supposed to fulfill? What happens if I believe my purpose is to be a great wife and my marriage ends in divorce; did I fulfill my purpose? If I find my life's purpose in being a devoted mother to my children, what happens when my children leave home and I encounter the empty nest? What happens if I decide that my purpose is to be a singer that is known across the world, and yet, I never obtain that dream? If I find my purpose in making a lot of money, what happens if I lose my job? Where will I find my purpose if I've been looking for it in things? If I do not have the "things" I've been seeking all along, what then?

Our purpose is not to make a lot of money. Proverbs 11:28 from The Message says it best this way: "A life devoted to things is a dead life, a stump; a God-shaped life is a flourishing tree." If I live each day trying to obtain my purpose without the understanding that I was created by God and for God, my life is going to be empty. When I look within the Word, I can find His promises, instructions, and His desires for me. Through His Word, I know that one of His purposes for my life is to do good works for Him. I love this verse from Ephesians:

> It is in Christ that we find out who we are and what we are living for. Long before we first heard of Christ and got our hopes up, he had his eye on us, had designs on us for glorious living, part of the overall purpose he is working out in everything and everyone. (Ephesians 1:11–12 MSG)

We do not need to live our lives in a state of despair and depression. Glorious living does not mean dreading each morning when the alarm goes off and feeling as if we just can't face another day because we don't find any purpose in the days we live. Living a gratifying and noble life filled with purpose is the kind of life God wants us to live. It isn't always easy to look beyond our own emotions in a tough situation, but that is what God asks us to do. Lay down your feelings and what you think and feel with your flesh—human nature—and look to Him to show you His purpose. Then follow His directions as He leads you to walk in them.

We can look to Jesus as our example. He lived to die. The Father sent him to speak for Him and be a witness for Him. Jesus said He did nothing on His own. "When you have lifted up the Son of Man, then you will know that I am he and that I do nothing on my own but speak just what the Father has taught me" (John 8:28 NIV). His purpose was to come and lead people to the Father through His sacrifice on the cross for our sins. Perhaps the time has come to follow His example by living and speaking only that which we have learned from Him. Fix your eyes on Him, knowing that He has a far greater purpose for your life than you could ever think or imagine!

There are going to be many times in our lives when we will have the opportunity to question, wonder, and doubt, but if we are going to change our identity, then we must always keep ourselves connected to God during those times. Remain consistent in the Word; don't run from it, as tempting as that is. Continue to be in fellowship with other believers and remain faithful to attending church. If you don't have a church, I encourage you to find one that teaches the Word and provides opportunities to grow with others through Bible study. God has a purpose for each one of us, and the trials and tests we go through in life can be used to glorify Him in our testimony. I once heard someone say our mess can be our message and our test can be our testimony.

Activate, Become, and Confess as you seek to change your identity one letter at a time.

## Activate - Start the Work

- Helen Keller said, "Many persons have a wrong idea of what constitutes true happiness. It is not attained through self-gratification, but through fidelity to a worthy purpose."[34] A great place to begin is to write out your definition of true happiness.
- Where have you found true happiness in your life as it currently stands?
- What do you think is missing from your life?

## Become – Come into Existence and #beYOU

- Read 3 John 1:2. What did John pray for his friend, Gaius to have?

125

- What do you think God wants for you? How does it align with your purpose?
- What is your responsibility in relation to what God wants for you?

## Confess – Declare in Faith

I am so loved by God that while I was still in my sin, Christ died for me. My friendship with God has been restored, I am His child, and my purpose is to glorify Him on this earth. I am not called to live according to the standard of the world, but to live according to the standard God has set. He has created me for His purpose, and I will seek that purpose for my life.

## Let's pray:

Father, You alone know the plans that You have for me—plans that give me hope for my future. I know that I sometimes make plans according to my limited understanding, but I only want to walk in step with Your plans for my life. Do not allow me to stray off of the path You designed for me but keep me focused on Your will and not my own. I trust You, Lord, because I was created by You and for You. I know this to be true. In Jesus's name, I pray. Amen.

# Q Is for *Qualified*

## God says I am QUALIFIED.

Giving thanks to the Father, who has *qualified*
us to share in the inheritance of the saints
(God's people) in the Light.
—Colossians 1:12 AMP, emphasis mine

**Qualified:** *having the qualities,
accomplishments, etc., that fit a person
for some function, office, or the like.*[35]

Years ago we met a couple from the church we were attending and became good friends. The husband is a lawyer and has his own practice. One day his wife told me that he had something he wanted to talk to me about, and I was surprised when he offered me a job to work in his office. I had worked as a secretary once before, but never for a lawyer. I was astonished at the offer since I had absolutely no paralegal training.

When I told him that, he simply said, "That's ok. I will teach you, and you can be trained in all that you need to know."

He had a need in his office for a secretary, and he saw qualities in me that he believed would be an asset to his business. He understood I was going to need time to learn and that there would be mistakes along the way. He was also aware of the time it would take before I understood all there was to know about the requirements of the job, especially pertaining to the law. With no qualifications at all for the job, he was willing to look beyond all that I lacked and look, instead, at the potential I had.

Isn't that exactly how God works with us? He sees beyond what we perceive as our lack and looks, instead, at what He knows is our potential. He knows that He has qualified us to do the work He has set before us!

The Scripture above and the word *qualified* made me think about the "saints in the light" the verse mentions. It caused me to stop and spend some time reflecting on just how *qualified* the men and women before us were—the ones that God used so mightily. What made the twelve disciples qualified to be the twelve disciples? What did Jesus see in these men that prompted Him call each of them to come and follow Him?

He saw two fishermen, brothers Simon Peter and Andrew, and then there was James and John, the sons of Zebedee, who were also fishermen. Matthew was a tax collector, and Simon was called a Zealot, which is a nice word for "religious fanatic."

Jesus even chose Judas Iscariot, the one who would betray Him, knowing he would betray Him.

Then I think about the Old Testament heroes of the Bible: Noah, Abraham, Sarah, Isaac, Jacob, Joseph, Moses, Deborah, David, Esther, Ruth, and others. These were men and women God chose and used for His specific purpose. Oh, how I would have loved to be with those who have gone before me and learned from them.

What do you suppose qualified each of the following men for the job God gave them? Noah built an ark, and yet I do not find anywhere in the Bible that says he was a master craftsman. Moses was chosen to lead God's people out of Egypt and yet he felt inadequate because he was "slow in speech" (Exodus 4:10). God called Abraham out from his father's home to a land that He would show him and then made a covenant with him, promising that He would make him into a great nation (Genesis 12:1-3). God chose David, a shepherd from the pasture, and promised him that his kingdom would last forever (2 Samuel 7:16).

We can see that God picked these men and used them, but I wonder what it was about them. What did they have in common? Then I discovered something in Hebrews 11—a little word with a powerful punch—*faith*. Hebrews 11 is called "the faith chapter" and it begins this way:

> Now faith is the assurance (title deed, confirmation) of things hoped for (divinely guaranteed), and the evidence of things not seen [the conviction of their reality—faith comprehends as fact what cannot be experienced by the physical senses]. (Hebrews 11:1 AMP)

I saw the thread that connected all of those men and women of the Bible with God—it was the thread of faith. Faith tied them all together, and faith can tie me to them! "For by this [kind of] faith the men of old gained [divine] approval" (Hebrews 11:2 AMP). They lived with dedicated passion for the Lord even though they couldn't see the outcome, and it won His approval.

What a faith builder Hebrews 11 is for us! Reading through the chapter, we see the writer reveals to us that it was by faith that God qualified each of them. As we look at the disciples that Jesus called to be fishers of men (Matthew 4:19), we see that they were people who we might view as men of great faith. But do you realize that those who had great faith also had times of great struggle?

Abraham and Sarah lied—not once, but twice—about their marital status to protect their safety. Sarah actually laughed at God when she first heard that she would bear a child in her old age (Genesis 18:12). Moses killed a man and hid the evidence (Exodus 2:12). David slept with a woman who was not his wife and then had her husband killed (2 Samuel 11). As a teen, Joseph seemed to have a bit of pride and was a tattletale, which provoked his brothers' hatred of him (Genesis 37). Peter rebuked Jesus, and then Jesus replied, "Get behind Me, Satan!" (Matthew 16: 22-23) and he also denied Jesus three times (Matthew 26). In fact, all but one of the disciples may have abandoned Jesus at the cross (John 19:25-27). And we know that Judas betrayed Jesus for thirty pieces of silver.

I often questioned my abilities and my rights as a Christian as I wondered how God could use me for His glory. How could I be "qualified" to carry His message of hope to those whom He brings into my path when I've made such a mess of my own life at times? How could I be, as the Scripture at the beginning of this chapter says, qualified "to share in the inheritance of the saints (God's people) in the Light."

I am not alone in believing the voice in my head that tries to convince me to get my act together before God can use me for anything. I have heard many people say that they just have too much "stuff" they must clean up before they'd be useful to God. Far too often we disqualify ourselves from allowing God to use us by looking through the lens of our past mistakes. It's an ugly truth that makes it easy to accept the lie that God could never possibly want to use us. I have heard it said by some, "Once I get things right in my life, then I will think about getting right with God." That isn't how it works. First, God wants us to get right with Him, and then He helps us get things right in our lives. That's when He qualifies us, when we allow Him to do the work!

We need to stop feeling inadequate, looking at our lack, and instead, embrace the fact that He desires to work through us. For many years, I stood behind what someone else said about the Bible, rather than what I read or believed, simply because I did not feel qualified to voice my opinion. I'd often say, "So and so says (fill in the blank) about the Lord," or "So and so says (fill in the blank) about the Bible."

One day while talking to a friend, she said, "I don't care what 'so and so' says; I want to know what *you* say."

It was difficult for me to believe that what I had to say had any importance. After all, what qualifications did I have when it came to knowing the Bible? We think that we need to attend Bible school or have some type of formal education before we share a verse of Scripture. We disqualify ourselves by look-ing at what we lack rather than acknowledging the power of God within us. God doesn't look for the person with the most degrees or trophies hanging on the wall. He looks for the most available. He looks for those who love Him and believe that He is able to do everything His Word tells us He can.

However, it is important for us to recognize that without Jesus we aren't qualified for anything, much less a life of eternity with the King of Kings and Lord of Lords! But He has qualified us to inherit the same life that the saints before us received. In

Isaiah 61 we learn about the power God gives when He qualifies his people:

> The Spirit of the Lord GOD is upon me,
>
> Because the LORD has anointed
> and commissioned me
>
> To bring good news to the humble and afflicted;
>
> He has sent me to bind up [the
> wounds of] the brokenhearted,
>
> To proclaim release [from confinement
> and condemnation] to the [physical
> and spiritual] captives
>
> And freedom to prisoners,
>
> To proclaim the favorable year of the LORD,
>
> And the day of vengeance and
> retribution of our God,
>
> To comfort all who mourn,
>
> To grant to those who mourn in Zion the following:
>
> To give them a turban instead of dust [on
> their heads, a sign of mourning],
>
> The oil of joy instead of mourning,
>
> The garment [expressive] of praise
> instead of a disheartened spirit.
>
> So they will be called the trees of righteousness
> [strong and magnificent, distinguished for
> integrity, justice, and right standing with God],
>
> The planting of the LORD, that He may
> be glorified. (Isaiah 61:1-3 AMP)

Your identity will change as you share your story! Tell everyone you meet the story of His grace in your life. Give God permission to use your story to help change the lives of those around you, regardless of how messy it is. Offer the mess to

Him, and allow Him to bring beauty from ashes. He wants to use your life and all you've walked through to speak into the lives of those around you. Share His love. Reach out with His kindness and grace. Offer the same mercy you were offered to each person He brings your way.

It's time to stop believing the lie that tells you, "You cannot be used by God because_____." You are qualified because you share in the inheritance of all the saints! They had a story to tell, too. Can you just imagine the day we meet in glory and we can sit around God's big banquet table and swap stories with the saints before us? Oh, what fun that will be! Practice up!

Activate, Become, and Confess as you seek to change your identity one letter at a time.

## Activate - Start the Work

- Read Hebrews 11. Make a list of each name and what the Bible tells us they did by faith.
- What do you learn from the faith examples of the saints?
- Which life do you find most relatable to your own?

## Become – Come into Existence and #beYOU

- Is there something from your past that keeps you from believing God has qualified you to serve Him? Acknowledge any lies that have prevented you from allowing God to use you for His purposes.
- Read Hebrews 13:8. What do we know to be true about Jesus?
- Now that you know you're qualified and called by God, what will you do to equip yourself for His service?

## Confess – Declare in Faith

I am strengthened with God's glorious power and will have the endurance and patience I need to step into the calling God has for me. I am filled with joy and will always thank the Father for this gift. God has qualified me to share in the inheritance that belongs to His people who live in the light. He has rescued us from the kingdom of darkness and transferred us into the Kingdom of His dear Son who purchased our freedom and forgave our sins (Colossians 1:11–14 NLT, paraphrased).

## Let's Pray:

God, forgive me for the unbelief that convinced me I was not qualified to step into the authority You have given me—I have held on to unbelief for far too long. Forgive me for listening to the lie that my past disqualifies me from the future You have planned for me. Help me to overcome any fear or religious thinking that would keep me bound in my old nature instead of my new nature in Christ. Amen.

# R Is for *Righteous*

God says I am RIGHTEOUS.

> He made Christ who knew no sin to
> [judicially] be sin on our behalf, so that in Him
> we would become the *righteousness* of God
> [that is, we would be made acceptable to Him
> and placed in a right relationship with Him
> by His gracious lovingkindness].
> —2 Corinthians 5:21 AMP, emphasis mine

**Righteous:** *characterized by uprightness or morality; acting in an upright, moral way; virtuous.*[36]

**Righteousness:** *the quality or state of being righteous.*[37]

Have you ever woken in the morning with one thought repeating in your brain? One Saturday morning, I awoke to the same statement running through in my mind: "It is time to put down the milk and start eating the meat." Over and over, I heard this thought repeat itself. While walking with my husband later that morning, we discussed some upsetting situations taking place within the church we attended at that time, and I shared with him the statement that would not leave my thoughts.

As we began to talk about it, we both began to feel that it was a message from the Lord, not only for us, but for the church as a whole. As we discussed how it pertained to the current circumstances we were walking through, we had a sense the Lord was telling us something very simple; it was time for His children to grow up! In other words, God wanted us to mature in the knowledge of the Word.

When I look back on that time, I have no doubt that is exactly what God was, and still is, calling us to do. Without question, God's desire and plan has always been for every person who calls on Him in faith to do the same. He wants us to mature in our faith and knowledge of who He is and what His Word actually says.

Paul wrote in his letter to the Corinthian church:

> Brothers and sisters, I could not address you as people who live by the Spirit but as people who are still worldly—mere infants in Christ. I gave you milk, not solid food, for you were not yet ready for it. Indeed, you are still not ready. (1 Corinthians 3:1–2 NIV)

In the book of Hebrews, we find this admonition:

> For though by this time you ought to be teachers [because of the time you have had to learn these truths], you actually need someone to teach you

again the elementary principles of God's word [from the beginning], and you have come to be continually in need of milk, not solid food. For everyone who lives on milk is [doctrinally inexperienced and] unskilled in the word of righteousness, since he is a spiritual infant. But solid food is for the [spiritually] mature, whose senses are trained by practice to distinguish between what is morally good and what is evil. (Hebrews 5:12–14 AMP)

Perhaps you are wondering what maturity has to do with righteousness. I had the same question when I first began to pray about the word for R. I wasn't sure if R should be redemption (the deliverance we received through Jesus's death) or righteousness. Each one holds such wonderful promises for us as we must learn to trust we are both redeemed and righteous. But, when we found ourselves in the middle of a conflict within our church, I sensed the Lord impressing upon me the greatest need at the moment was spiritual growth and maturity in the Lord. As I began to wholeheartedly seek to understand the following verse, I saw righteousness begin to form in my heart and mind.

He made Christ who knew no sin to [judicially] be sin on our behalf, so that in Him we would become the righteousness of God [that is, we would be made acceptable to Him and placed in a right relationship with Him by His gracious lovingkindness]. (2 Corinthians 5:21).

Look, once again, at this remarkable gift Jesus gave to us. It was for our benefit that He became sin. He did not just take our sin *on* Him—He *became* the sin. Can you imagine? The entire world's sin—past, present and future; He embodied all that sin. I cannot imagine how tormented He must have been with the

#BEYOU

weight of that on Him and within Him. He did it so we could become the righteousness of God. Amazing!

I love that 2 Corinthians 5:21 says that we might become the righteousness of God. We are the righteousness of God because Jesus Christ puts his righteousness on us; because that's what we *are*, that's what we portray to all those around us. It would be safe to say the righteousness of God has been *put on* us like an article of clothing. God put His righteousness on us when we accepted Jesus as our Savior and Lord. Now to the world around us, we reveal God's righteousness through our behavior, our speech, thoughts, and actions. We have the ability, because Christ made it possible, to be examples of Christ's righteousness because we *are* His righteousness.

How, then, do we begin walking in righteousness, and what does it look like? What steps can we take to make sure we grow and mature so we can be examples of Christ's righteousness? Here is something the Lord has shown me through my time with Him.

> Do not offer any part of yourself to sin as an instrument of wickedness, but rather offer yourselves to God as those who have been brought from death to life; and offer every part of yourself to him as an instrument of righteousness. (Romans 6:13 NIV)

First, offer yourself to God. Work on making Him number one in your life; that starts with studying His Word. I need the Word within me. Jesus said when confronted by Satan in the desert, "It is written: 'Man shall not live on bread alone, but on every word that comes from the mouth of God'" (Matthew 4:4 NIV). Just as we feed our physical bodies, we must feed our Spirits with the Word of God. Feed on the Word—actually, feast on it! Devour it as if it were your last meal!

It is so important that we know and understand the entire Bible, in its truth, to prevent deception at the hand of the Enemy. We will not live the abundant life Christ died for us to have if we allow the Enemy to steal the truth of the Word from us. We must take the entire Word as God's Word. Don't allow yourself to believe you can't understand the Word. God wants to share His heart with you, and he wants us to understand His Word.

Many people want to argue that the Bible isn't relevant for today or say they don't read it because they don't understand it. It absolutely is for today and every day after today! Hebrews 13:8 says, "Jesus Christ is [eternally changeless, always] the same yesterday and today and forever" (AMP).

This is why we need to attend a church that teaches the Word of God in its *full* truth. Find a solid Bible teacher to sit under for instruction. Proverbs 14:7 tells us to: "Go from the presence of a foolish man, When you do not perceive in him the lips of knowledge." When we know the Word for ourselves, we are able to discern if we are being taught the Word correctly. A good, solid Bible teacher will not be afraid of speaking hard things to those who are listening. Yes, our toes might get stepped on from time to time. But, better to be stung by the truth of God, rather than experience the painful sting of the consequences sin brings.

In the days in which we are living, it is imperative that we have clear instruction and that truth is taught from the pulpits in the churches. As we are taught from the Word, let's be willing to grow in the truth of the Word. When we grow, then we can influence others. Our example matters!

How can we be examples of righteous behavior to those around us? What comes out of our mouths can be a great place to start.

Do not let unwholesome [foul, profane, worthless, vulgar] words ever come out of your mouth, but only such speech as is good for building up others, according to the need and the occasion, so that it will be a blessing to those who hear [you speak]. (Ephesians 4:29 AMP)

I know there have been far too many times that I have allowed my mouth to be used for cursing rather than for blessing. It is amazing to me how much less I say if I keep a guard on my lips! What would happen if we talked about God's righteousness, His deeds, and His power, rather than the negative misdeeds of others? Now that we are God's righteous and redeemed, we care about how we live, and we give thought to our actions. Compromise is costly to a Christian.

Oh friends, let's become secure enough in our true identity, which is that of someone who has become *the righteousness of God*, so that we can get rid of all sin. Let's always ask God to help us behave in the same righteous manner in which He would. Psalm 23:3b says, "He leads me in paths of righteousness for his name's sake." It is for His fame and His glory, His name's sake, that we should allow Him to guide us in that path, not for ours. Let's make today the day we begin to change our identity by allowing His righteousness to flow through us and out to a world in need of His truth.

Activate, Become, and Confess as you seek to change your identity one letter at a time.

## Activate - Start the Work

- Read Proverbs 21:3. What is more acceptable than sacrifice? What are some examples of what this looks like in real life?
- When faced with the trials and tribulations of everyday life, how can we respond out of our righteousness rather than react out of our own human nature?

## Become – Come into Existence and #beYOU

- The definition of *righteousness* as translated from the Greek lists these words: integrity, virtue, purity of life, rightness, correctness of thinking, feeling, and acting. Take spiritual inventory and ask the Lord to reveal which of these might need some attention for you.

## Confess – Declare in Faith

"In the gospel the righteousness of God is revealed—a righteousness that is by faith from first to last, just as it is written: 'The righteous will live by faith'" (Romans 1:17 NIV). I live by faith, and I am more than able to live my life without compromise. I am blessed when I practice righteousness at all times (inspired by Psalm 106:3).

### *Let's Pray:*

Father God, David wrote that throughout his lifetime he had never seen the righteous forsaken by You (Psalm 37:25). Lord, turn my eyes to see what he saw. Help me to release any fear of what others will think when I choose to turn away from any unrighteous thinking, feeling, or doing in my life. My desire is to live as the righteous person I am in you. I pray in Jesus's name. Amen.

# S Is for *Secure*

## God says I am SECURE.

LORD, you alone are my portion and my cup;
you make my lot *secure.*
—Psalm 16:5 NIV, emphasis mine

**Secure***: free from or not exposed
to danger or harm; safe, in safe
custody or keeping, free from care;
without anxiety.*[38]

While visiting family for the Christmas holiday one year, I did my own little survey. I asked several of my family members these three questions: 1) How would you define secure? 2) What makes you feel secure? and 3) Where do people find security these days?

Every person answered the first question with the word "safe" in his or her answer. When people have a sense of safety, they feel secure. When threatened in any way, security is lost.

Relationships and finances were popular answers to question number two. We often find security in our relationships, our marriages, and our money. Our friends or spouses make us feel secure, and the more money we have in the bank, the more secure we feel.

As for the answers to the third question, there was a lot of variety. Some of those included: sex, drugs, alcohol, money, food, religion, material things, status, and popularity. It is true that we have many different options these days for what we can seek after in our quest for security.

For women, it's very easy to seek our security in our work, a man, or our friendships. Some will seek security in no one other than themselves because their trust has been mishandled and broken so often. I've had conversations with women and heard comments like, "I just have to do it myself because I cannot trust anyone else will do it." I have also known women at the other extreme who needed to have a man in their life or they felt completely lost. When one relationship didn't work out, they moved on to the next.

If we try to gain security from our friendships, we can become very possessive, to the extreme of becoming jealous when we have to share our friends with others. I remember my high school days and the drama that came from jealousy in friendships. I relived it all with my daughter and her high school days, too. Placing our security in our friendships will

tion or it, too, will not stand. In Luke 6:47–49, we are told
portance of a strong foundation:

> As for everyone who comes to me and hears my
> words and puts them into practice, I will show you
> what they are like. They are like a man building a
> house, who dug down deep and laid the foundation
> on rock. When a flood came, the torrent struck that
> house but could not shake it, because it was well
> built. But the one who hears my words and does
> not put them into practice is like a man who built
> a house on the ground without a foundation. The
> moment the torrent struck that house, it collapsed
> and its destruction was complete. (NIV)

ankfully, the Lord led us to wise counsel, and we were
 repair the wall for much less than we had been quoted.
rned the value of a strong foundation through the entire
s. A foundation that is properly built can withstand the
res that come at it from the outside. But one that is poorly
d improperly built can give a false sense of security, and
hen the troubles of life hit—and they can hit hard—there
ing there to hold you up.

d has proven Himself faithful time and time again. Why
doubt? True security is found here on earth when we have
undation planted firmly on the promises of the Word. No
 what the circumstance, God is more than enough. He
erything under control, and nothing is a surprise to Him.
 our foundation shakes we can say, "Well God, this wasn't
f my plan, but I know You are still in the midst of what
pening. Please show me where I will find You!" Psalm
says, "Our soul waits for the Lord; He is our help and our
." You can trust that God has a good grip on you and He's
tting you go. No matter what.

lead to heartache when life takes a turn or when the Lord
requires a move.

I, too, am guilty of trying to find security in friendships, in
money, in my marriage, in health, and in "things" only to discover that it never works. I have come to realize that when life
begins to get the best of me and I reach out for security, I'd best
be reaching for Jesus, or the thing I reach for may just be the
"thing" that ruins me.

Many of us find security in having lots of things, running up
large debts we could not possibly pay, spending money on the
best of everything, and making sure our families wear name-
brand clothing or do whatever activities they desire. We have
more things, opportunities, and money than our ancestors ever
had, yet statistics show that one in four women will experience
severe depression at some point in their life.[39]

I look around and I wonder, could it be possible that we are
looking for security in all the wrong places? Or maybe we just
don't understand what real security means. I've tried seeking
security in things and people. But I've come to realize that the
place I have found the most security is when I am standing on
the foundation of God's Word, the place of His promises, where
I can see myself the way He sees me.

When God brought the Israelites to the promised land, He
instructed Moses to send men to explore it and bring back a
detailed report of the land. What they found was, indeed, a
land flowing with milk and honey, grapes, pomegranates, and
figs. But what they also saw were the descendants of Anak,
Amalekites, the Hittites, the Jebusites, and the Amorites and
that's all it took to give a bad report to the children of Israel.

> Then Caleb quieted the people before Moses, and
> said, "Let us go up at once and take possession,
> for we are well able to overcome it." But the men
> who had gone up with him said, "We are not able

to go up against the people, for they are stronger than we." And they gave the children of Israel a bad report of the land which they had spied out, saying, "The land through which we have gone as spies is a land that devours its inhabitants, and all the people whom we saw in it are men of great stature. There we saw the giants (the descendants of Anak came from the giants); and we were like grasshoppers in our own sight, and so we were in their sight." (Numbers 13:30-33)

How they saw themselves and who they were in God's eyes were two very different things. God told them they could take the land He had given to them, but they refused to even try because with their own natural eyes, they were grasshoppers and unable to do it. We must be careful that when God has something that He wants us to possess we do not miss out on it because it looks bigger than what we think we are able to overcome.

When Joshua and Caleb tried to convince the Israelites that they could go into the land because God had given it to them, the people wanted to stone them. We can take on that attitude at times, can't we? When we are full of fear in a situation and someone walks in with a word of encouragement or hope, we would rather "stone" the person than find truth in his or her words. Having a strong foundation built upon the Word of God will help us when the storms of life come at us. We just need to make sure that our foundation isn't full of cracks.

One summer day, I was walking around the outside of our home when I noticed our foundation wall seemed to have a slight angle to it. I thought it looked very strange and mentioned it to my husband. He couldn't see it. I mentioned it to my parents when they were visiting. My mother saw it, but my father did not. So, we ignored it for months, until I was painting

the walls in our finished basement and n side wall did not feel right. I could see wha started my investigation.

I saw there was a bow to the wall an molding was pushed apart. I noticed tha cracked and moved. Finally, our worst fears we took the cover off of the area that holds foundation wall was cracked all the way do wall was actually resting against our water about an inch wide. From one end of the ho foundation wall had split and moved. The shifted the end wall. There was another h from top to bottom at the end of the house.

Once we discovered the cracked foun noticed walls within the house that were s stress. A crack here and there, a slight bo even the carpet in one of the rooms had be hadn't noticed these things before, but n our entire house was at risk because of the wall. We called contractor after contracto and couldn't find many willing to take on th "Too risky," they said.

These were the comments we heard c This became a huge concern to us because were willing to take on the job wanted th sands of dollars for the work.

We didn't have money, but we did hav to pray and ask the Lord to show us how H this all out.

While we were in the midst of prayin importance of a strong foundation. In the must be built on strong foundations if the and in the spiritual, our faith must also l

What a wonderful promise to hold on to. Our identity changes when we find our security in God alone. Our life is in His hands, and one day our time here on earth will end and we will spend all of eternity with Him in glory. I have a sign in my office with an acronym that spells out the word ALIVE. It says this: Always Living In View of Eternity. It reminds me to keep my feet planted on the foundation of God's Word and my eyes lifted to the One who knows how to handle every circumstance I face. Plant your feet and lift your eyes.

Activate, Become, and Confess as you seek to change your identity one letter at a time.

## Activate - Start the Work

- Where do you find security? What makes you feel insecure?
- Read Joshua 1:7–9. What are the instructions given here to Joshua that you could also apply to your life?
- What makes you prosperous? What brings success?
- Read Proverbs 10:9. How does integrity influence our security?

## Become – Come into Existence and #beYOU

- You will never be *secure* until you see yourself as God does. Do you view yourself as a grasshopper or a giant when it comes to what you sense God calling you to do?
- Find a friend who will remind you of your ability to conquer the "land" God has given you.

## Confess – Declare in Faith

I am building my foundation on the Rock of Jesus Christ. God has permission to remove anything, or anyone, from my life that

149

will cause me to sink, rather than stand firm. True security is not found in people, money, possessions, or power. My security is found in God and God alone. I will hold fast to Him and trust in Him when my plans fail.

## *Let's Pray:*

Father, You are my Rock and my Fortress and my Deliverer. You are the God of my strength; in You will I trust. You are a shield around me—my stronghold of safety and a refuge where I can find rest. Thank you, Lord, for providing me the security I need when my foundation is shaken—or even broken. You know my beginning from the end, and every one of my days has been written by You, for me. I trust You, Lord. You make my spiritual inheritance secure. In Jesus's name, I pray. Amen. (Inspired by 2 Samuel 22:2-3; Psalm 139:16, 16:5.)

# T Is for *Treasured*

God says I am TREASURED.

The LORD has declared today that you are his
people, his own special *treasure*,
just as he promised, and that you must
obey all his commands.
—Deuteronomy 26:18 NLT, emphasis mine

**Treasure:** *anything or person greatly
valued or highly prized.*[40]

I am fond of collecting old things. I enjoy browsing little antique stores, hunting for a treasure. While I hunt and pick up the items I find so interesting, my husband usually sits patiently somewhere waiting, but secretly praying he won't hear, "I want this!" I always remind him, "One man's junk is another man's treasure!"

As the Scripture from Deuteronomy rolled around in my heart, it made me think about that statement, "One man's junk is another man's treasure," and how it relates to friendship. It may seem odd to compare the two, but I've witnessed the pain people experience through broken relationships. It has caused me to spend time with the Lord praying for healing for those who have been hurt. It also has me wondering, "If we call ourselves friends, how is it possible for friends to treat one another so badly?" Too many times, I have seen the tears and heard the broken hearts as we try to understand how those closest to us could just walk away from a friendship.

Because the people in our lives do not always make us feel very treasured, I believe we can have a very hard time accepting that we are valued and treasured by God. There is such comfort for me, and I pray for you as well, knowing that we are never considered junk to God. He places great value on us; in fact, I happen to know that we are the apple of His eye—the delicate part of the eye that must be protected at all costs (Psalm 17:8).

He treasures everything about us. He treasures the time we spend with Him, our love for Him, and our friendship with Him. Unlike humans, who have a tendency to remove people from our lives rather easily, He never walks away from us. He doesn't get mad at us, doesn't hold grudges, and He doesn't hold our failures over us. He isn't easily offended, and He is always there for us. His promise is that He will never leave us nor forsake us (Deuteronomy 31:8; Hebrews 13:5). One Scripture I found encouraging is where Jesus calls me—and you—His friend:

> I no longer call you slaves, because a master doesn't confide in his slaves. Now you are my friends, since I have told you everything the Father told me. (John 15:15 NLT)

That statement is a great measure of friendship! He is willing to share everything He knows with us—His friends. Through the Word, we can learn so much about friendship. We can discover that His desire is for us to have friends and to understand why we need them. We can also discover what a good and healthy friendship should look like. It's true that everything He learned from His Father, He has made known to us.

Some of the deepest wounds I've carried came at the hands of people whom I considered to be my closest friends. I will tell you, too, that I know that I have also been the cause of pain to some of my friends, as well. I'm certain that most of the time the wounds we cause to others are unintentional. But, there are also times when, if we are honest, we know our intent is to cause suffering. We become upset, hurt, and angry and decide to exact our revenge.

Let's remember that Satan loves to steal, kill, and destroy; that's his job (John 10:10). He will do whatever he can to create tension in a relationship. If he can devastate someone through a broken relationship, he will try. As a roaring lion seeking to devour us, he will attempt whatever he can do to destroy and divide (1 Peter 5:8). That's why we have to be careful to not allow Satan to get a foothold in our relationships with one another. We must seek to know and understand how God works in our relationships and what He does behind the scenes in each one of us.

There is no doubt that God wants us to have good friends, just as He wants us to be a good friend. Scripture confirms this:

> Two are better than one, Because they have a good reward for their labor. For if they fall, one will lift up his companion. But woe to him who is alone when he falls, For he has no one to help him up. (Ecclesiastes 4:9–10)

God never intended for us to go through life alone. In fact, He said, "It is not good that man should be alone; I will make him a helper comparable to him" (Genesis 2:18). He gave Eve to Adam because He knew that it was not good to be alone. So, how can we be good friends? What does God desire for us to have in our friendships? The Word tells us if we want to have friends, we must first be a good friend. "A man who has friends must himself be friendly" (Proverbs 18:24a). We are warned, "The righteous should choose his friends carefully, For the way of the wicked leads them astray" (Proverbs 12:26). We also read in 1 Corinthians 15:33 that "bad company corrupts good character" (NIV).

Who we choose to have around us is very important to God, and it should be important to us. Being around others who are like-minded is also important. Paul tells us in Philippians 2:1–4:

> If you've gotten anything at all out of following Christ, if his love has made any difference in your life, if being in a community of the Spirit means anything to you, if you have a heart, if you care— then do me a favor: Agree with each other, love each other, be deep-spirited friends. Don't push your way to the front; don't sweet-talk your way to the top. Put yourself aside, and help others get ahead. Don't be obsessed with getting your own advantage. Forget yourselves long enough to lend a helping hand." (MSG)

In the early days of my faith walk, as I shared previously, I had an anger problem. I had a *big* anger problem. I remember reading a Scripture one day when I was really struggling with anger toward one of my friends. It's found in Proverbs, and the Lord used it to convict my heart. It says:

> Make no friendship with an angry man,
> And with a furious man do not go,
> Lest you learn his ways
> And set a snare for your soul." (Proverbs 22:24–25)

As someone who struggled with anger issues, I saw myself so clearly in this passage, and I realized that if my friends read those verses and obeyed them—like they should—they could easily tell me, "I must not go with you as a friend any longer. I may learn your ways and get caught in the snare of anger." (As I think on that now, maybe that's why I lost some of my friends!) It was always much easier for me to hold on to unforgiveness than to let people off the hook. I *was* a person who was easily offended. Do you know anyone like that?

We live in a society where people become easily offended. Just listen to the news every night and you can easily see who has been offended by something said or done by one person (or group) to another. People turn innocent statements upside down and inside out looking for a reason to be offended. Have we forgotten how to believe the best in one another? It isn't very often that you hear someone say, "I'm sure they didn't mean anything by it."

In our relationships, we need to believe the best about one another and overcome the tendency to be quickly hurt and easily offended. Friendships are destroyed when we cannot allow ourselves to forgive quickly, overcome the offense, and move on from it. "He who covers and forgives an offense seeks love,

But he who repeats or gossips about a matter separates intimate friends" (Proverbs 17:9 AMP).

I know from experience it is impossible to be in relationships that require you to watch every word you say and everything you do. I am not perfect, and sometimes—okay, often—I am going to slip up. I need my friends to understand that I mean no harm to them; I need them to believe the best of me. I need the people in my life to be willing to cover my sins with grace, love, and mercy.

If we want to have friends, then we will learn to be a good friend; that means letting go of things quickly, not taking offense often, and not keeping score. The battle begins right away when a careless word is spoken or a thoughtless act is done. Right then we can choose to either let it go or talk about it with the one who hurt us. Sometimes we can get over it without a word spoken, but there are times when hurts need to be taken care of.

If you have been hurt by someone and haven't been able to move beyond it, then chances are, you need to talk to them about it. Keeping things buried inside often will lead to an explosion of gigantic proportions that could have been prevented had the matter been discussed when it first happened. "The beginning of strife is like letting out water [as from a small break in a dam; first it trickles and then it gushes]; Therefore abandon the quarrel before it breaks out and tempers explode" (Proverbs 17:14 AMP). Be careful to not allow conflict to fester inside for too long. There is much damage done if we do.

There is an important lesson about friendship for us found in Exodus 33. In verse 11, we can see the intimate relationship God had with Moses, "So the Lord spoke to Moses face to face, as a man speaks to his friend." Good friends speak to one another face to face, not behind backs *about* one another. When we refuse to deal with our offenses toward one another, it becomes very easy to talk about the person you are upset with.

lead to heartache when life takes a turn or when the Lord requires a move.

I, too, am guilty of trying to find security in friendships, in money, in my marriage, in health, and in "things" only to discover that it never works. I have come to realize that when life begins to get the best of me and I reach out for security, I'd best be reaching for Jesus, or the thing I reach for may just be the "thing" that ruins me.

Many of us find security in having lots of things, running up large debts we could not possibly pay, spending money on the best of everything, and making sure our families wear name-brand clothing or do whatever activities they desire. We have more things, opportunities, and money than our ancestors ever had, yet statistics show that one in four women will experience severe depression at some point in their life.[39]

I look around and I wonder, could it be possible that we are looking for security in all the wrong places? Or maybe we just don't understand what real security means. I've tried seeking security in things and people. But I've come to realize that the place I have found the most security is when I am standing on the foundation of God's Word, the place of His promises, where I can see myself the way He sees me.

When God brought the Israelites to the promised land, He instructed Moses to send men to explore it and bring back a detailed report of the land. What they found was, indeed, a land flowing with milk and honey, grapes, pomegranates, and figs. But what they also saw were the descendants of Anak, Amalekites, the Hittites, the Jebusites, and the Amorites and that's all it took to give a bad report to the children of Israel.

> Then Caleb quieted the people before Moses, and said, "Let us go up at once and take possession, for we are well able to overcome it." But the men who had gone up with him said, "We are not able

> to go up against the people, for they are stronger
> than we." And they gave the children of Israel a bad
> report of the land which they had spied out, saying,
> "The land through which we have gone as spies is a
> land that devours its inhabitants, and all the people
> whom we saw in it are men of great stature. There
> we saw the giants (the descendants of Anak came
> from the giants); and we were like grasshoppers
> in our own sight, and so we were in their sight."
> (Numbers 13:30–33)

How they saw themselves and who they were in God's eyes were two very different things. God told them they could take the land He had given to them, but they refused to even try because with their own natural eyes, they were grasshoppers and unable to do it. We must be careful that when God has something that He wants us to possess we do not miss out on it because it looks bigger than what we think we are able to overcome.

When Joshua and Caleb tried to convince the Israelites that they could go into the land because God had given it to them, the people wanted to stone them. We can take on that attitude at times, can't we? When we are full of fear in a situation and someone walks in with a word of encouragement or hope, we would rather "stone" the person than find truth in his or her words. Having a strong foundation built upon the Word of God will help us when the storms of life come at us. We just need to make sure that our foundation isn't full of cracks.

One summer day, I was walking around the outside of our home when I noticed our foundation wall seemed to have a slight angle to it. I thought it looked very strange and mentioned it to my husband. He couldn't see it. I mentioned it to my parents when they were visiting. My mother saw it, but my father did not. So, we ignored it for months, until I was painting the walls in our finished basement and noticed that the outside wall did not feel right. I could see what was wrong when I started my investigation.

I saw there was a bow to the wall and that the chair rail molding was pushed apart. I noticed that the sheetrock had cracked and moved. Finally, our worst fears were realized when we took the cover off of the area that holds our water pipes. Our foundation wall was cracked all the way down the middle. The wall was actually resting against our water pipes, with a crack about an inch wide. From one end of the house to the other, the foundation wall had split and moved. The weight of it had also shifted the end wall. There was another huge crack that went from top to bottom at the end of the house.

Once we discovered the cracked foundation wall, we now noticed walls within the house that were showing signs of the stress. A crack here and there, a slight bowing in the middle, even the carpet in one of the rooms had been moving back. We hadn't noticed these things before, but now we realized that our entire house was at risk because of the broken foundation wall. We called contractor after contractor to look at the wall and couldn't find many willing to take on the job. "Too big," and "Too risky," they said.

These were the comments we heard over and over again. This became a huge concern to us because the contractors who were willing to take on the job wanted thousands and thousands of dollars for the work.

We didn't have money, but we did have faith. So, we began to pray and ask the Lord to show us how He was going to work this all out.

While we were in the midst of praying, He taught me the importance of a strong foundation. In the natural, our homes must be built on strong foundations if they are going to stand, and in the spiritual, our faith must also be built on a strong foundation or it, too, will not stand. In Luke 6:47–49, we are told the importance of a strong foundation:

> As for everyone who comes to me and hears my words and puts them into practice, I will show you what they are like. They are like a man building a house, who dug down deep and laid the foundation on rock. When a flood came, the torrent struck that house but could not shake it, because it was well built. But the one who hears my words and does not put them into practice is like a man who built a house on the ground without a foundation. The moment the torrent struck that house, it collapsed and its destruction was complete. (NIV)

Thankfully, the Lord led us to wise counsel, and we were able to repair the wall for much less than we had been quoted. We learned the value of a strong foundation through the entire process. A foundation that is properly built can withstand the pressures that come at it from the outside. But one that is poorly laid and improperly built can give a false sense of security, and then when the troubles of life hit—and they can hit hard—there is nothing there to hold you up.

God has proven Himself faithful time and time again. Why do we doubt? True security is found here on earth when we have our foundation planted firmly on the promises of the Word. No matter what the circumstance, God is more than enough. He has everything under control, and nothing is a surprise to Him. When our foundation shakes we can say, "Well God, this wasn't part of my plan, but I know You are still in the midst of what is happening. Please show me where I will find You!" Psalm 33:20 says, "Our soul waits for the Lord; He is our help and our shield." You can trust that God has a good grip on you and He's not letting you go. No matter what.

What a wonderful promise to hold on to. Our identity changes when we find our security in God alone. Our life is in His hands, and one day our time here on earth will end and we will spend all of eternity with Him in glory. I have a sign in my office with an acronym that spells out the word ALIVE. It says this: Always Living In View of Eternity. It reminds me to keep my feet planted on the foundation of God's Word and my eyes lifted to the One who knows how to handle every circumstance I face. Plant your feet and lift your eyes.

Activate, Become, and Confess as you seek to change your identity one letter at a time.

### Activate - Start the Work

- Where do you find security? What makes you feel insecure?
- Read Joshua 1:7-9. What are the instructions given here to Joshua that you could also apply to your life?
- What makes you prosperous? What brings success?
- Read Proverbs 10:9. How does integrity influence our security?

### Become – Come into Existence and #beYOU

- You will never be *secure* until you see yourself as God does. Do you view yourself as a grasshopper or a giant when it comes to what you sense God calling you to do?
- Find a friend who will remind you of your ability to conquer the "land" God has given you.

### Confess – Declare in Faith

I am building my foundation on the Rock of Jesus Christ. God has permission to remove anything, or anyone, from my life that

149

will cause me to sink, rather than stand firm. True security is not found in people, money, possessions, or power. My security is found in God and God alone. I will hold fast to Him and trust in Him when my plans fail.

## Let's Pray:

Father, You are my Rock and my Fortress and my Deliverer. You are the God of my strength; in You will I trust. You are a shield around me—my stronghold of safety and a refuge where I can find rest. Thank you, Lord, for providing me the security I need when my foundation is shaken—or even broken. You know my beginning from the end, and every one of my days has been written by You, for me. I trust You, Lord. You make my spiritual inheritance secure. In Jesus's name, I pray. Amen. (Inspired by 2 Samuel 22:2-3; Psalm 139:16, 16:5.)

# T Is for *Treasured*

### God says I am TREASURED.

The LORD has declared today that you are his
people, his own special *treasure*,
just as he promised, and that you must
obey all his commands.

—Deuteronomy 26:18 NLT, emphasis mine

**Treasure:** *anything or person greatly valued or highly prized.*[40]

I am fond of collecting old things. I enjoy browsing little antique stores, hunting for a treasure. While I hunt and pick up the items I find so interesting, my husband usually sits patiently somewhere waiting, but secretly praying he won't hear, "I want this!" I always remind him, "One man's junk is another man's treasure!"

As the Scripture from Deuteronomy rolled around in my heart, it made me think about that statement, "One man's junk is another man's treasure," and how it relates to friendship. It may seem odd to compare the two, but I've witnessed the pain people experience through broken relationships. It has caused me to spend time with the Lord praying for healing for those who have been hurt. It also has me wondering, "If we call ourselves friends, how is it possible for friends to treat one another so badly?" Too many times, I have seen the tears and heard the broken hearts as we try to understand how those closest to us could just walk away from a friendship.

Because the people in our lives do not always make us feel very treasured, I believe we can have a very hard time accepting that we are valued and treasured by God. There is such comfort for me, and I pray for you as well, knowing that we are never considered junk to God. He places great value on us; in fact, I happen to know that we are the apple of His eye—the delicate part of the eye that must be protected at all costs (Psalm 17:8).

He treasures everything about us. He treasures the time we spend with Him, our love for Him, and our friendship with Him. Unlike humans, who have a tendency to remove people from our lives rather easily, He never walks away from us. He doesn't get mad at us, doesn't hold grudges, and He doesn't hold our failures over us. He isn't easily offended, and He is always there for us. His promise is that He will never leave us nor forsake

us (Deuteronomy 31:8; Hebrews 13:5). One Scripture I found encouraging is where Jesus calls me—and you—His friend:

> I no longer call you slaves, because a master doesn't confide in his slaves. Now you are my friends, since I have told you everything the Father told me. (John 15:15 NLT)

That statement is a great measure of friendship! He is willing to share everything He knows with us—His friends. Through the Word, we can learn so much about friendship. We can discover that His desire is for us to have friends and to understand why we need them. We can also discover what a good and healthy friendship should look like. It's true that everything He learned from His Father, He has made known to us.

Some of the deepest wounds I've carried came at the hands of people whom I considered to be my closest friends. I will tell you, too, that I know that I have also been the cause of pain to some of my friends, as well. I'm certain that most of the time the wounds we cause to others are unintentional. But, there are also times when, if we are honest, we know our intent is to cause suffering. We become upset, hurt, and angry and decide to exact our revenge.

Let's remember that Satan loves to steal, kill, and destroy; that's his job (John 10:10). He will do whatever he can to create tension in a relationship. If he can devastate someone through a broken relationship, he will try. As a roaring lion seeking to devour us, he will attempt whatever he can do to destroy and divide (1 Peter 5:8). That's why we have to be careful to not allow Satan to get a foothold in our relationships with one another. We must seek to know and understand how God works in our relationships and what He does behind the scenes in each one of us.

There is no doubt that God wants us to have good friends, just as He wants us to be a good friend. Scripture confirms this:

> Two are better than one, Because they have a good reward for their labor. For if they fall, one will lift up his companion. But woe to him who is alone when he falls, For he has no one to help him up. (Ecclesiastes 4:9–10)

God never intended for us to go through life alone. In fact, He said, "It is not good that man should be alone; I will make him a helper comparable to him" (Genesis 2:18). He gave Eve to Adam because He knew that it was not good to be alone. So, how can we be good friends? What does God desire for us to have in our friendships? The Word tells us if we want to have friends, we must first be a good friend. "A man who has friends must himself be friendly" (Proverbs 18:24a). We are warned, "The righteous should choose his friends carefully, For the way of the wicked leads them astray" (Proverbs 12:26). We also read in 1 Corinthians 15:33 that "bad company corrupts good character" (NIV).

Who we choose to have around us is very important to God, and it should be important to us. Being around others who are like-minded is also important. Paul tells us in Philippians 2:1–4:

> If you've gotten anything at all out of following Christ, if his love has made any difference in your life, if being in a community of the Spirit means anything to you, if you have a heart, if you care— then do me a favor: Agree with each other, love each other, be deep-spirited friends. Don't push your way to the front; don't sweet-talk your way to the top. Put yourself aside, and help others get ahead. Don't be obsessed with getting your own advantage. Forget yourselves long enough to lend a helping hand." (MSG)

In the early days of my faith walk, as I shared previously, I had an anger problem. I had a *big* anger problem. I remember reading a Scripture one day when I was really struggling with anger toward one of my friends. It's found in Proverbs, and the Lord used it to convict my heart. It says:

> Make no friendship with an angry man,
> And with a furious man do not go,
> Lest you learn his ways
> And set a snare for your soul." (Proverbs 22:24-25)

As someone who struggled with anger issues, I saw myself so clearly in this passage, and I realized that if my friends read those verses and obeyed them—like they should—they could easily tell me, "I must not go with you as a friend any longer. I may learn your ways and get caught in the snare of anger." (As I think on that now, maybe that's why I lost some of my friends!) It was always much easier for me to hold on to unforgiveness than to let people off the hook. I *was* a person who was easily offended. Do you know anyone like that?

We live in a society where people become easily offended. Just listen to the news every night and you can easily see who has been offended by something said or done by one person (or group) to another. People turn innocent statements upside down and inside out looking for a reason to be offended. Have we forgotten how to believe the best in one another? It isn't very often that you hear someone say, "I'm sure they didn't mean anything by it."

In our relationships, we need to believe the best about one another and overcome the tendency to be quickly hurt and easily offended. Friendships are destroyed when we cannot allow ourselves to forgive quickly, overcome the offense, and move on from it. "He who covers and forgives an offense seeks love,

But he who repeats or gossips about a matter separates intimate friends" (Proverbs 17:9 AMP).

I know from experience it is impossible to be in relationships that require you to watch every word you say and everything you do. I am not perfect, and sometimes—okay, often—I am going to slip up. I need my friends to understand that I mean no harm to them; I need them to believe the best of me. I need the people in my life to be willing to cover my sins with grace, love, and mercy.

If we want to have friends, then we will learn to be a good friend; that means letting go of things quickly, not taking offense often, and not keeping score. The battle begins right away when a careless word is spoken or a thoughtless act is done. Right then we can choose to either let it go or talk about it with the one who hurt us. Sometimes we can get over it without a word spoken, but there are times when hurts need to be taken care of.

If you have been hurt by someone and haven't been able to move beyond it, then chances are, you need to talk to them about it. Keeping things buried inside often will lead to an explosion of gigantic proportions that could have been prevented had the matter been discussed when it first happened. "The beginning of strife is like letting out water [as from a small break in a dam; first it trickles and then it gushes]; Therefore abandon the quarrel before it breaks out and tempers explode" (Proverbs 17:14 AMP). Be careful to not allow conflict to fester inside for too long. There is much damage done if we do.

There is an important lesson about friendship for us found in Exodus 33. In verse 11, we can see the intimate relationship God had with Moses, "So the Lord spoke to Moses face to face, as a man speaks to his friend." Good friends speak to one another face to face, not behind backs *about* one another. When we refuse to deal with our offenses toward one another, it becomes very easy to talk about the person you are upset with.

Our social networks have become a way for us to expose our grievances about someone without ever facing them. It isn't always easy to go to a friend and talk to them about a hurt that you could not get over, but it is an act of love to do so.

I am indebted to the good friends who have been faithful to speak truth to me, no matter how painful it was to hear at the moment. Proverbs 27:6 is a Scripture that I have found comfort in and appreciated when used correctly! It lets us know this powerful truth: "Wounds from a sincere friend are better than many kisses from an enemy" (NLT). None of us is perfect, and we all have areas that need to be worked on. Our sincere and loyal friends aren't going to just allow us to do whatever and say whatever; they are going to hold us accountable. We know those who are in our lives that we can trust to tell us the truth, and sometimes the truth hurts!

There is a wonderful freedom that comes from a good word spoken at just the right time from a loyal friend. A wonderful characteristic of a good friend is just that—loyal. "A friend is always loyal, and a brother is born to help in time of need" (Proverbs 17:17 NLT). Another word for loyal is faithful, and a good friend is faithful, especially in times of need. There have been times in my life when my closest friends have known my need before I did. Sometimes I have been so broken by circumstances that I did not think I could ever be whole again. Yet God in His mercy sent a faithful friend to help in that time of need; it shows how much He treasures us.

I am thankful for friends who were able to see beyond my faults and into my heart, knowing that God was doing a work in me. Some stuck with me; others chose to walk away. I am grateful for those who forgave me when I messed up, and I appreciate how the Lord continually teaches me the art of forgiveness. I am also extremely thankful for the friendship we have in Jesus. What a friend He is. There is nothing like having a friend beside you to help you walk through the storms of life. Having loyal friends beside us is vital. However, changing our identity will move us to be a loyal friend to those God has put in our lives as well.

Activate, Become, and Confess as you seek to change your identity one letter at a time.

## Activate - Start the Work

- How would you explain your relationship with Jesus? Would you say He is a personal friend, acquaintance, or a religious figure to you?
- What barrier keeps you from knowing Jesus as a true friend?
- Read John 15:13. What did Jesus do for you, as a friend? How did this demonstrate how much he treasures you as a friend?

## Become – Come into Existence and #beYOU

- List three reasons why it matters who your friends are.
- Read about David and his friendship with Jonathon in 1 Samuel 18:1-4. What happened that gave them such a tight bond?
- Take inventory of your friendships. Who do you have that models a friendship like this? If you don't have a friend like this, ask the Lord to bring someone into your life who demonstrates self-sacrificing friendship. Remember to look for how you can be that kind of a friend too.

## Confess – Declare in Faith

I confess that I am not perfect but declare that I am willing to grow and become a better friend. I refuse to be swayed by emotion or misunderstanding in my relationships, and I will treat every friend as a *treasure* of God. I will seek understanding when I am hurt by words or actions and will refuse the devil's invitation to inflict pain on those who have hurt me.

## *Let's pray:*

Father, I want people in my life who are like-minded, have the same love for You, and are one in spirit and mind. Help me to remove selfishness from my life, as well as my desire to try to impress others. You want me to be humble and kind, thinking of others as better than myself. Help me Lord, to be the same friend to others as You are to me. Thank you for treasuring me enough to be my Friend. In Jesus's name, I pray. Amen.

# U Is for *Understand*

God says I am UNDERSTOOD.

Behold, God is mighty, and yet does
not despise anyone [nor regard any as trivial];
He is mighty in the strength and
power of *understanding*.

—Job 36:5 AMP, emphasis mine

**Understand:** *to be thoroughly
familiar with; apprehend clearly the
character, nature, or subtleties of.*[41]

I stood among other mourners in the line at a funeral home waiting my turn to sympathize with the family who had just suffered a great loss. I stepped forward, and as soon as the words began to slip through my lips, I knew. In my attempt to say the right thing to the father whose thirty-seven-year-old daughter had just passed away, I had failed. The tension was immense. My insides began to twist—as though a crank began to turn—followed by a conversation within my head. "Kolleen, you need to apologize – right now. Tell him you are sorry for asking an insensitive question."

My apology was quick. Overcoming my embarrassment, however, was not quick.

Some words are just better left unsaid. But there have been occasions when words rolled too quickly off my tongue because of a nervous need-to-fill-the-silence moment. Sometimes, they tumble out because of an insensitive I-didn't-think-first moment. Thankfully, I-don't-care moments happen less often than they used to. But, in my attempt to offer the right words at that moment I completely missed the mark.

For days following our interaction, I prayed the Lord would give them understanding of my heart's intent, rather than focus on the insensitivity of my words. It doesn't always happen though, does it? Misunderstandings take place when words are many; in fact, Solomon warned us that, "in the multitude of words sin is not lacking, but he who restrains his lips is wise" (Proverbs 10:19 MEV).

It isn't always easy to find the right words in the heat of someone's difficult moment. Just ask Eliphaz, Bildad, and Zophar. They were three of Job's friends who, in their desire to bring comfort to their friend, discovered their words had backfired. Once known as the greatest, wealthiest, and most respected man in the East, Job had suffered through great loss (Job 1-2). He was a changed man when his friends came to see him. Sorrow and suffering can do that to you. After hearing of his suffering, the three had traveled to mourn with Job and comfort him (Job 2:11). When they arrived, their own grief took over when they found their friend unrecognizable (Job 2:12).

In that moment, they did what good friends do. They sat beside Job, and for seven days and seven nights no one said a word (Job 2:13). Silence. It's a sacred, beautiful thing, but it can also be uncomfortable. Especially for someone who—like me—feels a heavy weight beneath too much silence. When the sound of silence becomes too loud, like Job's friends, I would eventually, find myself speaking words out of uneasiness, rather than thought.

This is when the "fixer" in me rushes in to try and save the day and do away with silence. Let's find the reason, discover the cause, and then move on to the remedy. But the words of my choosing may have a lasting effect on the one with whom I sit— and on me. When Job broke the silence and began to speak out of his heartbreak, his friends responded out of their "anxious thoughts" (20:2).

Eliphaz wanted Job to understand he was being disciplined for his sin. "Consider the joy of those corrected by God! Do not despise the discipline of the Almighty when you sin" (Job 5:17 NLT). Bildad wanted Job to repent. His, "if you . . ." statements cast blame on the very man God described to Satan as blameless (2:3). "God will not cast away the blameless," he said (8:20). In other words, "You're not so blameless after all, are you Job?" And Zophar felt Job needed to be rebuked and reminded that God was punishing him far less than he deserved (11:6).

Who needs to hear that when surrounded by sorrow and suffering? Unfortunately, for those who find themselves in a place of unexplainable suffering, our attempts to explain often lack compassion and understanding. Sometimes we simply need to concede that we won't always have the answers because we won't always understand.

Thankfully, however, there is One who does understand. God alone can completely understand each person's heart in the wake of suffering. And God alone can bring wholeness and healing once again to those who have become brokenhearted. "He heals the brokenhearted And binds up their wounds," the psalmist affirmed (Psalm 147:3). The Hebrew word for *bind* is *chabash* and can be translated to "bandage."[42] Can you imagine? Picture God bandaging your wounds. If you allow Him, that's just what He will do.

When we put a bandage on a wound, we cover the wound to protect it from infection. While the wound is covered, we cannot see the healing process that is taking place beneath the bandage, but we trust that it is happening. During the healing process, it might be necessary to take the bandage off, observe the healing process, clean the area, and change the bandage; however it's always best to leave a bandage on until the healing is complete. If we take the bandage off too early there is a chance that germs will get in the wound, and if that happens, infection might set in, which will make matters worse. If an infection, which is an infectious agent or contaminated material,[43] sets in, it takes much longer for the healing to be completed.

God's healing work is similar; He is the bandage that covers our wounded hearts. We may not see the work being done underneath the surface, but we should trust that He is there, doing what only He can do, restoring as only He can restore. If we refuse to allow Him to complete the healing work He desires, infections are sure to set in. Infections such as: bitterness, anger, resentment, cynicism, depression, and confusion. He knows the pain of suffering, and as the Great Physician, He wants to heal every wound that has the potential to infect our hearts with contaminants that seek to destroy our relationship with God and relationships with one another. The only possible way this can happen is if we allow Him full access to our pain. And that takes trust. It will probably take someone with a good listening ear, too.

I find great comfort from Job 36:5 that lets me know nothing in our life is trivial to God and "He is mighty in the strength and power of understanding" (AMP). To fully understand someone, we must be thoroughly familiar with them, and we know that God is intimately acquainted with all of our ways (Psalm 139:3). He understands us when others can't. Or won't.

I imagine Job found comfort when his friends sat down beside him. I've certainly appreciated when friends have gathered around me when I've needed surrounding. However, Job's friends failed to remain steadfast in honoring God throughout the trial. We can learn so much from their time together. When they arrived, Job's friends did not recognize him in his time of grief. Job had just lost everything except for his wife, and he was covered in boils and grief. You may not recognize your friend in their time of sorrow and suffering. Give yourself permission to simply sit with them amid the silence without trying to fix anything.

Next, Job explained his heartbreak: "If my misery could be weighed and my troubles be put on the scales, they would outweigh all the sands of the sea. That is why I spoke impulsively" (Job 6:2-3 NLT). Friends in the midst of sorrow and suffering may speak impulsively. Grief isn't always expressed neatly or nicely. Give one another the freedom to speak without patrolling every word.

And lastly, let's not jump to conclusions on why this is happening. Job said, "Stop assuming my guilt" (6:29 NLT). Before Job entered into this test God described him "as blameless—a man of complete integrity (Job 1:8 NLT). At the end of the test, the Lord had rebuked each one, but Job was the only one God said spoke accurately of Him. In their need to fill the silence with opinion, the friends spoke inaccurate assumptions (Job 42:7).

"One should be kind to a fainting friend, but you accuse me without any fear of the Almighty" (Job 6:14 NLT). When our friends feel faint because of grief and sorrow, they need our kindness and prayers. Don't bring accusations, opinions, or words to fill the silence. Find comfort in the silence.

And if you believe you have no one to sit beside you in your struggle, remember you have Jesus. He suffered in every way so you would never be able to say, "He does not understand what I am going through." He is the only One thoroughly familiar with every wound you carry. He knows all about your pain and knows how it's possible to overcome the battle of hopelessness.

Changing our identity begins the moment we run into the arms of Jesus to find the comfort and understanding we've been searching for. Remember, nothing to Him is trivial; it all matters. But more importantly, you matter.

Activate, Become, and Confess as you seek to change your identity one letter at a time.

### Activate – Start the Work

- Read Isaiah 53:1-6. In our effort to be understood, we often fail to understand. What do you understand about Jesus?
- How do you feel about the idea that Jesus understands our sorrow and grief?
- What do you wish other people would understand about you when you're hurting?

## Become – Come into Existence and #beYOU

- I saw a meme one day that read, "Texting: a brilliant way to miscommunicate how you feel, and misinterpret what other people mean."[44] How have you experienced this?
- What action steps could you take to avoid misunderstanding someone else or being misunderstood?

## Confess – Declare in Faith

When I feel misunderstood, I will run to Jesus because I know He understands me. When my heart is wounded and bruised, I will allow the Holy Spirit to shine His spotlight on the wound and place His bandage of healing over the hurt. I will allow the Lord to do His work to bring complete healing.

### *Let's Pray:*

Lord, You alone can bring ultimate healing to every wound within my heart. Jesus, You understand me more than I even understand myself sometimes, and You can bring those into my life who can help me find healing from the trauma and pain. I surrender myself to You, and when I am whole, use me to help others find the same healing. I pray in Jesus's name. Amen.

# V Is for *Victorious*

## God says I am VICTORIOUS.

For everyone born of God is *victorious* and
overcomes the world; and this is the *victory*
that has conquered and overcome the
world—our [continuing, persistent] faith [in
Jesus the Son of God]. Who is the one who is
*victorious* and overcomes the world? It is
the one who believes and recognizes the fact
that Jesus is the Son of God.

—1 John 5:4–5 AMP, emphasis mine

**Victorious:** *having achieved a
victory; conquering; triumphant.*[45]

Several years ago, a local school asked me if I would work as a one-on-one aide for a student who had difficulty making good decisions. He was a great kid who just could not (or would not) follow the rules. He was constantly reprimanded by his teachers, sent to the principal's office, and quite frequently endured both in and out of school suspension. Once I began working with him and got to know him, I saw him far differently than those who saw him as a troublemaker and a "bad kid." I saw a young man who needed to know that he was able to make better choices. I saw a young man who needed to know that not everyone had given up on him.

So many people in his life were weary and didn't know how to handle him anymore. He had been given up by his birth mother and placed in foster care. He moved from different foster homes and was later adopted, but his adoptive parents couldn't handle his rebellion, and in their weariness had all but given up on him. I could see he was full of anger and resentment, but what I also could see was a desire for someone to have his back. He ached for someone to come beside him and help show him what the better options were. He really wanted to find someone who would love him, accept him, and teach him.

One morning, as we were sitting on the bus together, he talked with me about his future. We discussed what life could possibly hold for him. I remember asking him what he wanted to be doing in five years. His answer was that he hoped he wasn't in jail.

Oh, how my heart broke for him. I looked at him and said, "You know, if you always do what you've always done, you will always get what you've always got." Someone once shared that nugget of truth with me and it changed my life.

It was time for him to see that if he wanted to stay out of jail and turn his life around, then he had to stop doing what he had always done and try a new approach to life. It was time to put away the actions that were always getting him in trouble and respond differently to situations in life.

I can relate to that—how about you? Have you ever responded to situations in your life and discovered that maybe, just maybe, you needed a "time out" for incorrect behavior? I know I have. Far too many times actually. And I have learned through the loving correction of a merciful Father that if "I always do what I've always done, I will always get what I've always got."

The Bible reminds me that God wants far more for me, for you too, than a life full of despair and defeat. His Word is full of good promises for us. He has already enabled us—by His Holy Spirit—to live a victorious life. Contrary to what the devil whispers to us and many believe, we are able to overcome the battles we endure in our life.

It was no different for God's people, the Israelites, when they were living as slaves to the Egyptians. God didn't want them to live as slaves in Egypt; He intended for them to be set apart for Him. Unfortunately for the Israelites, however, although they saw God do incredible miracles to get them out of Egypt, they could never fully leave Egypt. They always had Egypt in the back of their minds. Whenever life got tough out in the desert, they begged to go back—even though it had been a life of slavery. Aren't we all like that at times? When we become uncomfortable waiting for the promised land to come, we decide life was simpler back in Egypt. We choose to go back to the familiar thing rather than move on to the place that requires faith to obtain.

Why? Because in the familiar we are comfortable. We know what's expected of us there. It's less scary than something completely new to us, even though the familiar may be the unhealthiest place for us to be. When the Israelites stood at the Red Sea and realized that Pharaoh was chasing them, fear took over.

> As Pharaoh drew near, the sons of Israel looked, and behold, the Egyptians were marching after them, and they became very frightened; so the sons of Israel cried out to the LORD. (Exodus 14:10 NASB)

This was their cry:

> "Is it because there were no graves in Egypt that you have taken us away to die in the wilderness? Why have you dealt with us in this way, bringing us out of Egypt? Is this not the word that we spoke to you in Egypt, saying, 'Leave us alone that we may serve the Egyptians'? For it would have been better for us to serve the Egyptians than to die in the wilderness." (Exodus 14:11–12 NASB)

Now, fear itself is not sin and I don't blame them for having fear at the sight of their enemies closing in on them; they were trapped with the sea in front of them and the slave drivers closing in on them. There was no place to escape. But, had they actually told Moses before to leave them alone so they could continue as slaves? I don't recall that verse. I do, however, recognize what happened: fear exposed their mindset. They'd always run back to their slave way of thinking every time they were challenged by something hard—until they changed how they saw themselves.

I recognize this because I've lived it. I've been challenged by the decision: remain a slave to my victim mindset or follow the Lord's commands into a life of victory.

Meanwhile, while the Egyptians were moving closer to the Israelites:

> Moses said to the people, "Do not fear! Stand by and see the salvation of the LORD which He will accomplish for you today; for the Egyptians whom you have seen today, you will never see them again forever.

The LORD will fight for you while you keep silent."
(Exodus 14: 13–14 NASB)

We must stop running back and learn, instead, to stand still as we wait . . . and watch . . . and trust what the Lord can and will accomplish for us. When was the Lord fighting for them? In their silence. So, how should we compose ourselves while the Lord fights for us? Remain silent.

Ouch. Silence has never come easy for me—especially in the midst of discomfort. It's much easier to grumble and complain about the unpleasant situation I'm experiencing than it is to keep silent!

However, standing still will require that I remember the Lord already has a battle plan prepared for my victory. I just need to wait for Him to show me, and the first step toward the win will be changing the pattern of my behavior. Speaking the Word of God in faith over our battles reveals the power of God, and it allows Him to go to work. The trouble is we have become so accustomed to looking at our problems that we forget to look to Him as our Help, our Strength, and Source of wisdom. We become victims to our problems rather than victorious over our problems.

How do we know if we're stuck in a victim mindset? Check your conversations. If you talk about the same struggle year after year without change, you're stuck. When we refuse to forgive someone for a wrong against us, we become the victim. We are a victim when we refuse to listen to the counsel or advice that can help move us forward but instead choose to continue in our old habits. How can we expect to have a victory over a situation if we always talk with negativity and believe that it can never change?

God has a different approach. Stop talking.

It's okay to use your past as a place of reference, but God never intended for it to become a place of residence. There does come a time when we have to let things go because God wants us to move forward, always growing and changing.

Finally, the Lord said to Moses, "Why are you crying out to Me? Tell the sons of Israel to go forward" (Exodus 14:15 NASB). I love that verse. It's like the Lord said, "Don't just stand there and cry; do something!"

Battles are hard, and victories don't come easy. We need to be careful to not allow ourselves to become victims on the way to becoming victorious. God leads us to a victory through a course of events and circumstances that He knows will bring about the change He looks for in us. He is able to bring good out of bad, beauty from ashes, joy instead of mourning and change that will last (Romans 8:28; Isaiah 61:3). Opportunities arise every day, and we will need to choose between victim or victor. We may believe that we have every right to be the victim, and that very well may be true.

There are a lot of people who have become victims through no fault of their own. In fact, you may be one of them. Ugly things might have happened in your life that have left you broken and victimized. Know that God takes the victimization of His children very seriously. Psalm 10:14 says, "But you, God, see the trouble of the afflicted; you consider their grief and take it in hand. The victims commit themselves to you; you are the helper of the fatherless" (NIV).

The greatest victory you can have is when you no longer live as a victim but release everything to the Lord for Him to take care of. Through Christ we absolutely can place those who have wronged us in His hands to deal with them, no longer bound to the pain of it. Think of this: He went to the cross for those who wronged Him too.

If you don't see the victory in your life right away, your first inclination might be to run back to Egypt. I'd like to encourage you to remain steadfast in the battle. Do not allow the Enemy to fill you with fear, but march on to the victorious life God has waiting for you. We can overcome the world and live wonderful, victorious lives because we believe in Jesus Christ, and through Him we can overcome any obstacle thrown at us.

Let's go out together and become victors instead of victims. We can change our identity when we refuse to hold on to the belief that we have a right to live as a victim because of what was done to us. Choose to live your days on earth knowing that you can overcome anything because He has enabled you through His Son to do it. Are you ready to do battle? I am.

Activate, Become, and Confess as you seek to change your identity one letter at a time.

## Activate - Start the Work

- Ask the Lord to expose which of these character-istics your mindset and actions reveal in relation to your beliefs about yourself: are you a victim or victor?
- What do you need to release to Him once and for all so you can move forward in *victory*?

## Become – Come into Existence and #beYOU

- Following the Red Sea escape, the Israelites sang a song to the Lord. Read Exodus 15. How did they describe the Lord in verse 2?
- When was the last time you felt like singing because you experienced victory and freedom through God's demonstration of power?

- To become a victor, you're going to need to know the power of God within you. Who is the Lord in verse 3?

## Confess – Declare in Faith

"For the word of God is living and active and full of power [making it operative, energizing, and effective]. It is sharper than any two-edged sword, penetrating as far as the division of the soul and spirit [the completeness of a person], and of both joints and marrow [the deepest parts of our nature], exposing and judging the very thoughts and intentions of the heart" (Hebrews 4:12 AMP). Jesus was victorious over sin and death, and because of Him, I can be too. I will no longer be held captive to a victim mindset. Instead, I will see a victory!

## Let's Pray:

Father, I do not want to spend one minute more than I need to wandering around in the wilderness. If I think like a victim, show me. Forgive me if I blame others for my trip there. Help me to forgive _____ for the hurt that started my journey into the desert. Show me what victory looks like—through You—and help me trust in You to move me into the promised land You have planned for me. Amen.

# W Is for *Wise*

God says I am WISE.

For the LORD gives *wisdom*; From His mouth come knowledge and understanding.
—Proverbs 2:6, emphasis mine

**Wise:** *having the power of discerning and judging properly as to what is true or right; possessing discernment, judgment, or discretion.*[46]

**Wisdom:** *the quality or state of being wise; knowledge of what is true or right coupled with just judgment as to action; sagacity, discernment, or insight.*[47]

One of my less-than-desirable personality traits is my temper. As a very young and immature Christian, I could fly off the handle as quick as you could snap your fingers! It is an ugly, embarrassing truth. I remember one instance when we were expecting company for the weekend, and my grandmother was visiting for the first time. She had never flown before, but after my grandfather's death she decided that it would be the right time to experience it.

I was very excited to have her and my mother come for a few days. But, as I prepared for their arrival, I became more and more, well . . . stressed. There were loads of laundry to be done, meals to prepare, groceries to be bought, kids to be taken care of, etc. The list was long as I wanted everything to be perfect for her arrival.

As I went about the day checking the finished tasks off my list, I decided to add the lawn to the list. It needed mowing, and it needed mowing, *right now*. Now, my sweet husband, who had been working twelve-hour nights, was trying hard to get some sleep. I believe I had gone in once or twice and "gently" tried to wake him to remind him that there was a lot to be done in a few short hours. The kids were making a mess as fast as I could clean it up, and now, the lawn *needed* mowing, too. Well he didn't get up at my command, so that was one more thing I added to my list. I eventually decided to march out to the garage and take matters into my own hands.

That was not the wisest decision. I was mad.

After all, I was "the *only one* who cares about things around here!" and I was "the *only one* working to get things done around here!"

We had a push mower at the time, and the more walking I did, the madder I became. It wasn't too long before I was stomping along pushing that mower with such force, I must have looked ridiculous to the neighbors. I was practically running and pushing the mower.

As I mowed, I came to an extension cord that ran about 20 feet across the yard to the house. I am not sure why all sense of wisdom left me at that moment, but we don't make the wisest decisions when we're mad, do we? I bent over, grabbed that extension cord and pulled it out with all the force of my anger.

In amazement and horror, I stood and watched as the plug of the electrical cord came back at me from twenty feet away like a mad snake and smacked me right in my lower lip, leaving behind prong marks and a nice gash in my lower lip.

My, oh my, how the lip does bleed!

With my hands over my mouth, I ran into the house. Pat had no choice but to get up now; we needed to go to the emergency room!

Due to the large crowd at the hospital, I couldn't get the stitches in my lip before my grandmother's plane arrived. So, I went to the airport with ice on my big fat lip, greeted Grandma and my mother, and then went back to the E.R. for four stitches. Embarrassing? Just a little. Lack of wisdom? Maybe a lot.

I could share one story after another of moments when wisdom has been lacking in my decision-making and the consequences have been less than stellar. If you think about it, most of our regrets come from decisions that lacked wisdom on our part. Financial crises happen because we aren't wise with our money. We may lose job opportunities because we are unwise in our actions at work. We experience hurt in relationships because we don't use wisdom in choosing relationships. Our health deteriorates when we aren't using wisdom in the care of our bodies. The list goes on and on.

Every area of our life requires us to make wise decisions if we are going to live a life full of God's blessings. We find wisdom and gain a heart of understanding when we hold tightly to one principle of the Word. True wisdom is found in the fear of the Lord, and understanding is found when we let go of sin. Often, we do not want to let go of our sin, and we become so casual in our relationship with the Lord that we no longer hold the proper fear, or reverence, for Him. As I gained a deeper understanding of who God was, I began to view Him more "fearfully."

The word *fear* is taken from the Hebrew word *yir'ah* and translates to: "to revere and respect."[48] To fear God properly is to respect and reverence Him. We walk in wisdom when we walk in the fear of the Lord. We may be faithful church attendees and faithful in our tithes and offerings, but if we have no reverence for God in our daily lives, we are not wise.

Living in reverence for the Lord means living with the awareness that He sees everything we do. Our respect for Him ensures that we live to please Him and bring honor and glory to Him. If my behavior will not bring honor to Him, then I need to seek Him for wisdom and understanding on what will.

James tells us that we can go to God and ask for wisdom and it will be given to the one who asks. "If any of you lacks wisdom, you should ask God, who gives generously to all without finding fault, and it will be given to you" (James 1:5 NIV). That is exactly what King David's son Solomon did when he inherited the throne from his father. He must have understood the importance of wisdom, because when the Lord offered him anything he wanted, he asked for the Lord's wisdom.

> At Gibeon the LORD appeared to Solomon in a dream by night; and God said, "Ask! What shall I give you?" And Solomon said: "You have shown great mercy to Your servant David my father, because he walked before You in truth, in righteousness, and in uprightness of heart with You; You have continued this great kindness for him, and You have given him a son to sit on his throne, as it is this day. Now,

O LORD my God, You have made Your servant king instead of my father David, but I am a little child; I do not know how to go out or come in. And Your servant is in the midst of Your people whom You have chosen, a great people, too numerous to be numbered or counted. Therefore give to Your servant an understanding heart to judge Your people, that I may discern between good and evil. For who is able to judge this great people of Yours." (1 Kings 3:5–9)

Solomon chose to ask for a gift of far greater use than riches and honor. He asked for an understanding heart. That request so pleased the Lord, He promised that Solomon would not only have a wise and understanding heart, he would also have what he didn't ask for—riches and honor (1 Kings 3:10–13).

Can you imagine? The entire earth's population wanted to sit and listen to him speak because they knew he spoke the wisdom of God. But even with his wisdom, Solomon had a weakness for women. 1 Kings 11:3–4 tells us that Solomon took many wives for himself, and it turned his heart from the Lord. Solomon's lack of control over his desire for woman cost him the kingdom.

God had given Solomon the wisdom that no man had ever possessed before, but he allowed his desire for women to overrule his obedience to the Lord. Have we allowed our own desires to ever overrule our obedience to the Lord? Sure we have! What have you lost when you couldn't control yourself and disobeyed God? Solomon lost his kingdom. What was your kingdom? A marriage lost because of unfaithfulness? Your health lost due to alcoholism or drug abuse? Your savings lost from a gambling addiction?

How have you lost your kingdom?

I have allowed myself to make many foolish decisions because I didn't want to wait on the Lord. I have spoken a word too soon and hurt people. I have spent money foolishly on items I didn't need or on ideas I thought were going to be great investments that didn't work out. I have had to ask the Lord to forgive me for the times I ignored His counsel and wisdom and did my own thing. But I know that He forgives, and He uses everything for His glory. Nothing is ever wasted with God if we surrender it all to Him. I wonder if Proverbs 3:5-8 came out of this experience for Solomon.

> Trust in the LORD with all your heart and lean not on your own understanding; in all your ways submit him, and he will make your paths straight. Do not be wise in your own eyes; fear the LORD and shun evil. This will bring health to your body and nourishment to your bones. (NIV)

We have God's wisdom available to us as we pray and request it, but we must put it into action, or it will cost us. If you have not prayed asking God to give you wisdom in making your decisions, I encourage you to do so. Living in the days in which we do, we need to have God's wisdom and understanding to guide us and protect us.

Let's remember that true wisdom, the wisdom we need to help us live the full life God has for us, is found only through God, and He has given us His Word to teach us. Let's read it and let it soak deep into our hearts and minds so we can truly walk in the wisdom He has given us.

Wisdom is the only word that we have studied thus far that requires us to ask for it. All others are given to us when we accept Christ. Our identity will change when we sincerely ask God for it. What are you waiting for? Let the asking begin!

The following is an acronym the Lord gave me to help follow His voice of wisdom. I pray it helps you too.

**W** – Wait. Don't move too fast. "The wisdom of the prudent is to give thought to their ways, but the folly of fools is deception" (Proverbs 14:8 NIV).

**I** – Increase in knowledge of the Word, which will "make me wiser than my enemies" (Psalm 119:98 NIV).

**S** – Seek the advice of godly counsel. "Where there is strife, there is pride, but wisdom is found in those who take advice" (Proverbs 13:10 NIV).

**D** – Delight in wisdom! "A fool finds pleasure in wicked schemes, but a person of understanding delights in wisdom" (Proverbs 10:23 NIV).

**O** – Obey the voice of wisdom, which can save me from making foolish decisions. "Do not forsake wisdom, and she will protect you; love her, and she will watch over you" (Proverbs 4:6 NIV).

**M** – Mature in understanding God's Word and His wisdom. "And Jesus increased in wisdom and stature, and in favor with God and men" (Luke 2:52).

Activate, Become, and Confess as you seek to change your identity one letter at a time.

## Activate - Start the Work

- Proverbs explains the consequences of rejecting God's wisdom. What can we learn from Proverbs 1:20–33?
- What have you experienced personally when you have tried to ignore the voice of wisdom?
- What safety have you experienced when you have listened?

## Become – Come into Existence and #beYOU

- Read James 3:13–18. If you are wise and understand God's ways how will your actions demonstrate it?
- How will you know if you are not wise?
- What do you find the most challenging to obey and apply from those verses?

## Confess – Declare in Faith

The *wisdom* from above is first of all pure. It is also peace loving, gentle at all times, and willing to yield to others. It is full of mercy and the fruit of good deeds. It shows no favoritism and is always sincere. And those who are peacemakers will plant seeds of peace and reap a harvest of righteousness (James 3:17–18 NLT, paraphrased). I will seek the Lord for His wisdom.

### Let's Pray:

Father God, please fill me with the wisdom You are so willing to share—the same wisdom You gave to Solomon. Lord, I desire to make decisions with my life that will bring You glory and honor. Your wisdom will protect me. Your wisdom will keep me on the right path. Bring wise people around me, because those who walk with the wise will be wise (Proverbs 13:20). I pray in Jesus's name. Amen.

# X Is for *Excluded*

God says I am EXCLUDED.

Blessed are you when men hate you,
And when they *eXclude* you, And revile
you, and cast out your name as evil,
For the Son of Man's sake.
—Luke 6:22, emphasis mine

**Excluded:** *to shut or keep out; prevent
the entrance of. To expel and keep out;
thrust out; eject.*[49]

I'm sure you wondered if I would find a word that begins with the letter X. Actually, so did I! I prayed about it, and thankfully, the Lord gave me a bit of creative help! I asked the Lord to reveal which word He was interested in having me study and write about. What did He want us to know and understand? When my eyes fell upon *exclude,* I had a strong sense that this might be the word, but I second-guessed myself! After all, being excluded doesn't sound very uplifting or encouraging, does it?

Then I began to read through the Gospels about the life of Jesus, and I realized that if ever there was a person who understood exclusion, it is Jesus. After all, He didn't get many invitations from the religious people, did He? Once He began to challenge them in their teachings and their understanding of God, the meetings they had together were about Him and how they could get rid of Him. They weren't interested in becoming friends with Him. In fact, He really pushed their buttons.

He was excluded from the "Religious Leader Club" because He wasn't afraid to challenge the people living around Him with the truth. There is much to be learned from reading about the life of Jesus. He knew the truth because He *was* the Truth and He freely shared it with everyone, regardless of how He might be perceived or viewed by them. He didn't mind stepping on a few toes here and there along the way. He just lived His way, knowing what His purpose was, and not worrying what people thought of Him. He spent His time doing the work of the Father, regardless of how others assumed He should spend His time.

He had His priorities in order, and following the crowd of the day was never important to Him. Helping the crowd was.

Jesus was able to show us how to live in the world and not be part of the world. He knew that it would be a challenge for us to do the same, so He prayed for us. In John 17 Jesus prayed to His Father for His disciples, and we are included in that prayer:

> "I do not pray that You should take them out of the world, but that You should keep them from the evil one. They are not of the world, just as I am not of the world. Sanctify them by Your truth. Your word is truth." (John 17:15–17)

It was never God's intention for us to *not* live in the world. Jesus didn't ask God to remove all of His disciples and place them in the "All Inclusive Club for Christ." Rather, He prayed that God would keep us from the Evil One. Jesus understood the trials that we would experience while living in this world. But who is the Evil One?

We've talked about him before but let's really look at who he is. His name is Satan and he is our adversary, the devil. He opposes God and he opposes us. If we are going to walk in the blessings that God has for us and live the life God intended for us to live, then we must recognize the Enemy and know how to defeat him. We can no longer pretend that he is not real and not a threat to us, or the world we live in.

The children's book, *The Berenstain Bears and the Truth,* has a great poem on the inside cover. It reads:

> No matter how you hope,
> No matter how you try,
> You can't make truth
> Out of a lie.[50]

As I survey our world and the system of morals and values that grows farther and farther away from God's standards, I cannot help but think of the truth that comes from the Berenstain's poem. We may not want to acknowledge it, but we live in a world that has slipped so far away from the principles that God intended for us to live, that we now strive to get truth out of lies.

The reality of it is you can hope and you can try, but you cannot get truth out of a lie. No matter how badly I want to believe something to be true, if it goes against the Word of God, it is a lie. If you are trying to live in a way that contradicts Scripture and you're telling yourself it's okay, you are being deceived to accept a lie as truth. That's exactly what the Evil One wants us to do. He wants us to twist the Word of God or be too afraid of what others may think if we really live the way the Word tells us to live.

Honestly, it is no easy task for Christians to live in a world that is hostile toward Christ. However, we have the Word of God that can give us insight into how to defeat our enemy at his own game. Let's take a look at our enemy, the Evil One, and see what the Word has to say about him and most importantly about the authority believers have over him to make it possible to live in the world.

The Word of God reminds us that we can overcome the Enemy who desperately wants to take us down: "You are of God, little children, and have overcome them, because He who is in you is greater than he who is in the world" (1 John 4:4). One of the most important truths we need to have is the understanding that the Holy Spirit who is in us is far greater than the devil and all his cohorts. But without the faith to believe this, the devil is going to whip us in battle every time.

Once we understand that the Holy Spirit is in us, we must realize that revelation comes by the Holy Spirit. We will never understand the authority of the believer with our own understanding; it is only through the power of the Holy Spirit that this can happen. How did we get the authority to overcome the devil? God Himself has given us the authority to overcome him because we are His children and we belong to Him.

Authority is power God has delegated to us—His power—to overcome and defeat the devil. Let that sink in. Satan is obligated to recognize our authority, and he has to flee when we command him. We must change our thinking process! I cannot tell you how many times I have listened to my fellow believers in Christ talk of all the work Satan was doing in their life while never once mentioning what God was doing. We need to honor what Jesus went to the cross for. He overcame the power of hell.

Satan thought he had won, but Colossians 2:15 tells us what actually happened: "And having disarmed the powers and authorities, he made a public spectacle of them, triumphing over them by the cross" (NIV). Believers remain hostage to Satan when they fail to understand and live in the victory Jesus won for them on that cross. When we proclaim Christ's victory in our lives, we will then have the ability to overcome the devil, ungodly desires, and wrong thinking.

If we are going to be victorious Christians as God has planned for us, then we must use the tools He has made available to us. Learn to speak out of faith and put your faith in what the Word of God says and promises. In Ephesians 6 we have clear instructions for how to do spiritual battle. We are told to "put on all of God's armor so that you will be able to stand firm against all strategies of the devil" (Ephesians 6:11 NLT). Yes, he has strategies and he has schemes, but God has given us the power to overcome and defeat any of the Enemy's schemes. He has prepared us by revealing to us that we have been given all the protection we need:

> Therefore, put on every piece of God's armor so you will be able to resist the enemy in the time of evil. Then after the battle you will still be standing firm. Stand your ground, putting on the belt of truth and the body armor of God's righteousness. For shoes, put on the peace that comes from the Good News

so that you will be fully prepared. In addition to all of these, hold up the shield of faith to stop the fiery arrows of the devil. Put on salvation as your helmet, and take the sword of the Spirit, which is the word of God. Pray in the Spirit at all times and on every occasion. Stay alert and be persistent in your prayers for all believers everywhere." (Ephesians 6:13–18 NLT)

I've never appreciated being excluded. I don't like to miss anything! But over the last few years, I have come to realize that I want God's blessings more. I want Him to pour out His blessings on my life and my family's lives. I know that with this blessing comes the exclusion that may come as a result of standing firm as a follower of Christ. I began to look at who He blesses and I discovered this: "Oh taste and see that the Lord is good; Blessed is the man who trusts in Him" (Psalm 34:8).

We can change our identity and desire a blessed life as we learn to trust in the Lord. Let's lean in and put all of our doubts and fears to rest in His arms. A blessed life is a life that has the right fear, or reverence, for the Lord. A changed life is a life that no longer lives in fear of the Evil One and isn't afraid to be eXcluded.

Activate, Become, and Confess as you seek to change your identity one letter at a time.

## Activate - Start the Work

- Do you struggle with exclusion? How does it make you feel when you are excluded?
- Are you willing to be *excluded* from cliques and circles for the sake of your faith? What makes this challenging for you?

## Become – Come into Existence and #beYOU

- What are our instructions from James 4:7 when it comes to the devil?
- What action steps will you take in obedience to this verse?
- What patterns of thinking will you replace to change from a mindset of defeat when it comes to the Evil One to a mindset of full authority to resist him?

## Confess – Declare in Faith

"If the Good News we preach is hidden behind a veil, it is hidden only from people who are perishing. Satan, who is the god of this world, has blinded the minds of those who don't believe. They are unable to see the glorious light of the Good News. They don't understand this message about the glory of Christ, who is the exact likeness of God" (2 Corinthians 4:3–4 NLT). I will no longer allow the Enemy to blind my mind. Jesus, I will look for You in every situation.

### Let's Pray:

Father God, I want to see You and live my life according to Your truth. Open my eyes to see the deception of the Evil One. Where I have been misled, lead me on the right path. Where he has caused blindness to prevent me from living in the fullness of blessing You intend, give me sight. He is sneaky; Lord, give me discernment to recognize him. Help me see myself as the person You created and no longer live tied to the lies of the Enemy. He wants me weak in my faith, but You have delegated Your power to me. Give me understanding to use it correctly. I pray in Jesus's name. Amen.

# Y Is for *Yoked*

God says I am YOKED with Jesus.

"Come to Me, all who are weary and heavily
burdened [by religious rituals that provide no
peace], and I will give you rest [refreshing
your souls with salvation]. Take My *yoke* upon
you and learn from Me [following Me as
My disciple], for I am gentle and humble in
heart, and you will find rest (renewal, blessed
quiet) for your souls. For My *yoke* is easy
[to bear] and My burden is light."

—Matthew 11:28–30 AMP, emphasis mine

**Yoke:** (Noun) *something that couples
or binds together; a bond or tie.*
(Verb) *to be or become joined, linked,
or united.*[51]

D o you ever find yourself wondering what it would have been like to live during Jesus's time on earth? I do. Sometimes I wonder which crowd I would have stood with. I also find myself wondering how Jesus had compassion for the very people who would betray Him and ultimately kill Him.

I pondered what the Lord would want us to learn as we near the end of this #beYOU journey together. As we change our identity one letter at a time, what nugget of truth does He have for us still to discover that will change how we see ourselves, and Him, for the rest of our lives?

As I thought about how Jesus responded to those who betrayed and killed him, I wondered what we could learn from him. And then I saw a glimpse of His desire for us in Jesus's statement, "Take My yoke upon you and learn from Me" (Matthew 11:29). Don't you truly want to learn from Jesus? I yearn to know all there is to know about Him so I can be more like Him. Perhaps, learning from Jesus requires learning how to wear His yoke of compassion.

In the Gospels, there are numerous times we are given a glimpse of His compassion when Jesus was with multitudes of people, and then we discover the circumstance behind His compassion. For example, He often saw the people and was moved with compassion and healed sickness and disease. In one instance, He was moved with compassion for the multitude that had been with Him for three days and had nothing to eat. He didn't want to send them away hungry, so with seven loaves of bread and a few fish, He fed them (Matthew 15:32–39). In Matthew 9:36 we see how He "was moved with compassion for them, because they were weary and scattered, like sheep having no shepherd. So, He began to teach them many things."

I love the compassion of Jesus. It was that very heart of compassion that saved my soul! It is His heart of compassion that sees the needs of the people and is moved to help meet them.

I'm sure that it must have been out of His heart of compassion that He spoke the words from Matthew 11:28, "Come to Me all you who labor and are heavy laden." He said this to the Jewish people who were suffering under a heavy load of burdensome rules put on them by the religious leaders of the day. Rules, rules, and more rules. The excessive rules of the religious leaders brought oppression rather than freedom. They were experts in law-keeping, but it seemed the laws they expected others to obey they might not have been keeping themselves.

> Then Jesus said to the crowds and to his disciples: "The teachers of the law and the Pharisees sit in Moses' seat. So you must be careful to do everything they tell you. But do not do what they do, for they do not practice what they preach. They tie up heavy, cumbersome loads and put them on other people's shoulders, but they themselves are not willing to lift a finger to move them. "Everything they do is done for people to see: They make their phylacteries wide and the tassels on their garments long; they love the place of honor at banquets and the most important seats in the synagogues; they love to be greeted with respect in the marketplaces and to be called 'Rabbi' by others." (Matthew 23:1–7 NIV)

What a tragedy to be told to obey everything they teach, but not to do as they do. He called them hypocrites for speaking one thing and doing another (vs. 13 NKJV). He also called them "blind guides" who were like whitewashed tombs (vs. 16). Seems rather harsh, doesn't it? After all, these were the spiritual leaders. But Jesus knew that they were in it for the wrong reasons. They liked the power, the fame, and the money that their position brought them. Rather than drawing people to God, Jesus saw that they were causing people to be bound by religious rules.

Let's talk about hypocrisy within the church of today. I know people that don't go to church because of the hypocrisy within it. Many people are crushed by the failures of leaders within the church when a secret sin is brought to light. It brings great disillusionment to a place that was supposed to be safe and secure. After all, this is the church, the one place you thought you could trust. There are still churches today that follow the traditions of men and leave Jesus out. When you have man-made rules without the relationship of Jesus, you will have rebellion. I heard Andy Stanley say once in a message, "Rules without relationship lead to rebellion."

We live in a culture that rebels against God because people have only seen Him through the eyes of man-made rules. Rules that miss the important aspect of the personal relationship that God intended and desired to have with His children. The hypocrisy—the play-acting and fake religiosity—isn't anywhere near what Jesus intended for the church.

Jesus quoted Isaiah 29:13 from the Old Testament when he spoke to the scribes and Pharisees, "These people draw near to Me with their mouth, And honor Me with their lips, But their heart is far from Me. And in vain they worship Me, Teaching as doctrines the commandments of men" (Matthew 15:8–9). Would He have the same thing to say to us today? I'm afraid He might. How many go to church on a Sunday morning simply to check off the box of obligation?

That's exactly what Jesus saw when He walked into the lives of the multitudes around Him. When Jesus looked at them, He saw sheep without a Shepherd, and I ask myself, why? They had spiritual leaders, didn't they? They had the law of Moses as a standard for life. Why were they so lost? They were lost because they were just going through the motions, working to obey the law out of obligation and without any passion or love for it. It was just a duty and a ritual they had to follow in obedience to the Jewish leaders and customs. The Jewish people had the Messianic prophecies to look to in expectation of Jesus's arrival, yet they did not recognize Him for who He was when He walked among them.

"He was in the world, and the world was made through Him, and the world did not know Him. He came to His own, and His own did not receive Him" (John 1:10–11). Do we suffer the same blindness within our own churches at times today? We have the Word of God—Words of Life—which reveals the truth of God's gift of grace, yet are we so stuck on our traditions that we don't recognize Him moving among us? Consider this warning about man-made traditions:

> "Beware lest anyone cheat you through philosophy and empty deceit, according to the tradition of men, according to the basic principles of the world, and not according to Christ." (Colossians 2:8)

Jesus is calling out, "Come to me, all you who are weary and burdened, and I will give you rest" (Matthew 11:28 NIV). We need to rest from religious works and legalistic rules; to make this possible He offered us His yoke. When you put a yoke on oxen, you take two stubborn animals and bind them together. They are now a hard-working team, walking side by side, no longer going in separate directions. Where one goes, the other goes. Jesus wants us to put on a yoke that binds us with Him so that where He leads, we obediently walk right along beside Him. We accept His will above our own and don't stubbornly fight to be separate from the yoke or pull in the opposite direction.

Jesus said that His yoke is easy and His burden is light. How is it easy? Evangelist and theologian, Charles Finney, explains it this way:

> His yoke is easy because he never prohibits any-thing, and never imposes upon us any restraint

except for our own good, or for the good of the race to which we belong. If at any time he restrains us, or deprives us of anything that we would like, it is love's restraint. He sees that it would be injurious to us, injurious to the world, and consequently dishonorable to him; and therefore enlightened love compels him to restrain us.[52]

If He puts a yoke on us that withholds nothing except that which will cause harm to us—or harm to the world or His name—why do we fight against the yoke? Many times it's because we have lost the love and we honor Him with lips only, having hearts that are far from Him.

Oh, we may do good works believing that if we work hard enough and are good enough, then that should be enough. What, then, do we do with this verse from Ephesians: "For by grace you have been saved through faith, and that not of yourselves; it is the gift of God, not of works, lest anyone should boast" (Ephesians 2:8-9). Today, many people live out a faith based on works, and because of the "law," they are tied to heavy yokes of bondage. Taking off the yoke of religious works and putting on the yoke of Jesus is much more appealing. While putting on the yoke of Jesus does require action, it's an action based on love. Sometimes we can become so busy worshipping our "works" within the church that we forget Who we are really there to worship.

Based on my own experience, I want to help you understand that when you allow Him to place His yoke on you and you sense the freedom, you will love to serve Christ. You will never want to do anything that would cause harm to Him or His Name. You will find such joy in living a surrendered life to Christ you can't help but want to dance in worship, lift your hands in praise, and thank Him for the remainder of your days! So, I ask you, have you allowed Christ to place His yoke on you? Are you yoked to Him? Are you weary and worn out on religion, or have you found the joy in a full relationship? If you are weary and ready to change your identity, Jesus is calling to you. "Come to Me . . . I want to give you rest." Don't wait another minute.

Activate, Become, and Confess as you seek to change your identity one letter at a time.

## Activate - Start the Work

- Consider your relationship with Christ. Have you found religion, or true faith through a personal relationship with Jesus? Jesus changes your life when you give Him access to your heart.
- If you have been a believer in Christ for a long time, list some of the ways you have found comfort and rest in being yoked to Him.
- If you are trying to live in your own efforts, what do you need to surrender to Him to be *yoked* to Him?

## Become – Come into Existence and #beYOU

- Jesus was always motivated by love. Would you say you lean toward living more by the law of legalism, or do you believe you are motivated by love? How have you grown in love as you have matured in your relationship with Jesus?
- Read Romans 7:1–6. What does verse 4 reveal to us about our relationship with Christ?
- What does it mean to "bear fruit," or produce a harvest for God?
- What does verse 5 tell us about the kind of "fruit" that our old law-bound nature could produce?

- Describe what the freedom explained in verse 6 means to you. How is living by the Spirit different from the way you used to live?

## Confess – Declare in Faith

I cannot be made right with God by trying to keep the law. It is only through faith that a righteous person has life. This way of faith is very different from the way of the law, but Christ has rescued me from the curse of the law. I am saved by my faith in Jesus Christ. I refuse to live according to the mandates of men (inspired by Galatians 3:10–13).

## *Let's pray:*

Lord Jesus, I want to be yoked to You. I am weary of religion. I am tired of trying to be good enough or kind enough. Please teach me how to be led by the Spirit so that I may be more like You. Give me Your heart of compassion and help me to see others in the same way You see them. Help me to never forget that I, too, was once stuck in bondage to the law before I discovered freedom in You. I want Your yoke, Jesus. Put it on me now. I pray in Jesus's name. Amen.

# Z Is for *Zealous*

God says I am ZEALOUS for Him.

As many as I love, I rebuke and chasten.
Therefore be *zealous* and repent.
—Revelation 3:19, emphasis mine

**Zealous:** *full of, characterized by, or due to zeal; ardently active, devoted, or diligent.*[53]

The news is never lacking for stories about individuals or organizations who are zealous for a cause they believe in. Some we may agree with, and some we may not. There have been times when I have understood the passion and reasoning, while at other times it has made no sense at all to me. But, when I think back to nearly twenty years ago, when the Lord opened my spiritual eyes to Him, I know that there were those who understood my passion while there were also those to whom it made no sense at all. I became very zealous, to say the least. I had so much passion and excitement for the Lord that I thought everyone should feel and believe the same way I did.

It made for some pretty miserable days in my life because not everyone wanted to hear what I had to share. Not everyone wanted to do what I thought they should do, and most importantly, not everyone was going to believe how I thought they should believe. I have a tendency to get really excited over the things of God. When I see God move in a situation I've been praying about, or I recognize how He's spoken to my heart, I get really excited. And sometimes in my excitement, I become zealous. I like the dictionary definition, *ardently active*. It means "intensely devoted."

I am zealous when I gain a new revelation of understanding within His Word, and not only can it be hard to keep up with me, it might be hard to understand me. I have had to learn to be very careful in my zeal because sometimes I have said and done things that have had more of a negative effect rather than a positive one. I believe that can be true for any of us, and I believe it's important for us to watch for the tendency.

We have all heard stories of religious groups, Christian groups included, who have said and done things out of zeal that do not reflect positively on God's nature or character. Their zealous nature can often lead to unwise or unethical actions and decisions—ones that don't well represent our faith. I cannot help but wonder if this verse found in Proverbs isn't a verse that we should embrace a little more tightly: "Do not let your heart envy sinners, But be zealous for the fear of the Lord all the day" (Proverbs 23:17).

It's important to be zealous for the Lord, and I believe that God, indeed, wants us to be zealous for Him, but our zeal must be *in* the fear of the Lord. If we have the proper fear, or reverence of the Lord, in our zeal for Him, it will prevent us from misunderstanding and wrongfully interpreting the Scriptures. It's too easy to take Scripture out of context and adjust it to say what we *want* to hear rather than what we *need* to hear. Paul told Timothy in a letter that this would happen. "For the time will come when men will not put up with sound doctrine. Instead, to suit their own desires, they will gather around them a great number of teachers to say what their itching ears want to hear" (2 Timothy 4:3 NIV).

Oh, we must be so careful to interpret the Word of God as it was intended and not misuse it by taking Scriptures out of the context in which they were written. We are led astray when we try to take the Word and change it fit to our desires rather than allowing the truth of the Word to change us to fit God's desires for us. God never intended for us to make His Word comfortable for us to hear. We must be challenged by it; it should convict us to change! When Peter wrote his second letter, this was his opening greeting: "Grace and peace [that special sense of spiritual well-being] be multiplied to you in the [true, intimate] knowledge of God and of Jesus our Lord" (2 Peter 1:2 AMP).

That is exactly what Peter wanted for those who read his writings—correct and precise knowledge of God and of Jesus. He wanted people to know the Father, Son, and Holy Spirit and correctly understand everything about them. If I wrote a letter to one of my kids with instructions for them to carry out, I would want them to interpret the letter as I intended it, not twist my words and decide they were going to interpret it however they saw fit. If there was something they couldn't quite figure out, I would want them to look at my character, who I am, and all I stand for to determine what I meant. If it made them a little uncomfortable while reading it, I would hope they would understand I had their best interest in mind when I wrote it. We must be precise and correct in our knowledge of the Word and in our understanding.

You may ask: as we change, aren't we supposed to be zealous for the Lord? Absolutely. But a lesson I learned along the way was the importance of balance. We must be careful to remain balanced in every area of our lives, even in our walk with the Lord. We are told that as Jesus grew, He "increased in wisdom and stature, and in favor with God and men" (Luke 2:52). God used this verse to show me the key areas in my life where balance must be found: physical, mental, social, and spiritual. If one of these areas is lacking attention, I am out of balance.

> Be sober [well balanced and self-disciplined],
> be alert and cautious at all times. That enemy of
> yours, the devil, prowls around like a roaring lion
> [fiercely hungry], seeking someone to devour.
> (1 Peter 5:8 AMP)

Balance is a huge area in our lives where I see that Satan really likes to play around. If he can get us off balance in one area, then he knows we will be off in other areas as well, especially in our walk with the Lord. For example, if we get off balance in our work and become a workaholic, then he knows our family will suffer. If he can get us off balance in our eating and exercise, then he knows our health will suffer. And if he knows he can get us off balance in our thinking and understanding of the Word of God, then our witness to the world will suffer. When Satan schemes to get people out of balance in the

Word and off of God's course for their lives, there may be a lot of zeal, but is it correctly placed?

The word *zealous* from Revelation 3:19 comes from the Greek word *zēloō*, and one of its definitions is "to be zealous in the pursuit of good."[54] While being zealous for God and wanting to defend and uphold Him and His teachings is right, God desires for us to be balanced in living our lives in such a way that it draws people to Him and doesn't turn them off to Him. How we behave determines how people are going to view God.

When I discovered that being zealous for the Lord also meant being zealous in the pursuit of good . . . wow! What an eye-opener that was. Jesus said, "For out of the abundance of the heart the mouth speaks. A good man out of the good treasure of his heart brings forth good things, and an evil man out of the evil treasure brings forth evil things" (Matthew 12:34–35). The good treasure within me is the Word of God, and it brings forth good things. I can be zealous in the pursuit of good by allowing the Word of God to dwell within me and using it as a guide to help me live a well-balanced life—one that brings honor and glory to Him.

People are watching God's children. When they see us, do they see a God of love and compassion, or a God that is demanding and harsh? Do they hear love and devotion when you speak of Him, or do they hear rules and condemnation? We can be balanced in our speech; it takes practice.

It amazes me how easy it is for us to allow ourselves to speak the unkind words, words that tear down, rather than the words that build up. Jesus said that if we don't have a good treasure within our hearts, then evil is brought forth. If we had the "good treasure" of the Word dwelling richly within us and zealously pursued good, our treatment of others might look a little different. We might not be so quick to send that text message of hateful words. We might think twice before posting our grievances on social media. We just might find that we are able to overlook offenses or forgive a little quicker.

Let the love in our hearts and the thankfulness we feel for Christ be shared with zealousness but also reverently and with proper fear and respect of the Lord. We have to be careful that we aren't so worried about what others think that we don't share anything about Christ when He presents an opportunity for us.

If we are to reach out to people with the hope of Jesus Christ, then we must believe in the hope of Jesus Christ. If we are going to reach people with the love of Jesus Christ, then we must emulate the love of Jesus Christ. We can't give to others what we really don't have in ourselves. Zeal comes out of our love for Christ and all that He has provided for us. Let's be careful to remain well balanced in all areas of our lives, but especially in our walk with the Lord and in our understanding of His Word.

As we change our identity, let's live *zealously*, pursuing good so others can see Jesus. It is a wonderful thing to be zealous for the Lord and all He has provided for us. My desire is to live my remaining days here on earth knowing that I had the proper zeal for the Lord, that my knowledge of Him was correct, and that because of it, others wanted to know more about Him. Will you join me?

Activate, Become, and Confess as you seek to change your identity one letter at a time.

## Activate - Start the Work

- How would you describe a zealous person? Are you one? Who do you know that you would consider zealous?
- How do people get off track in their zeal for God?

- What are some other areas in life where we can get off track while meaning well?
- Is there anyone to whom you need to make amends because you got a bit carried away in your zeal?

## Become – Come into Existence and #beYOU

- In what way do you think God wants to shape you so you represent His name in a positive light to people who encounter you in everyday life?
- Of the four areas in our lives: mental, physical, spiritual, and social, which one would you say is the most balanced? Which is the least balanced?
- What is lacking from each of these areas for you?
- What can you do to make sure all areas are equally balanced?

## Confess – Declare in Faith

God, you have not given me a spirit of timidity or cowardice or fear, but You have given me a spirit of power and of love and of sound judgment and personal discipline. I have the abilities that will result in a calm, well-balanced mind and self-control (inspired by 2 Timothy 1:7 AMP). I know who I am in You! I am accepted, no matter what I have done or where I've been. I am beautiful to behold through the eyes of my Father. I have been changed—no longer the same as I once was. I am desired by the God of the universe. I have been established, forgiven, and made free. I am God's child and because of that I am holy—made in His image. I am justified from my sins. I am known and loved. I have been given the mind of Christ and have been made new—able to overcome. God has given me a purpose! I am qualified by God to share in His inheritance. I am righteous and secure; nothing can separate me from Him. I am treasured, understood, and victorious—full of wisdom, excluded from the world, and yoked to the King of Kings and Lord of Lords. I am now able to live a *zealous* life in the joy of the Lord.

## *Let's pray:*

Father God, please help me to understand Your Word in the manner in which You wrote it. Wherever I am out of balance in comprehending the intent of Your Word, please give me a clear revelation. Whatever I need to do to gain correct interpretation of Your Word, show me. Thank you for giving me zeal for You and a love for Your Word. Now, please make sure I have balanced it in a manner that honors You. Thank You for the work You have done in shaping my identity. Continue the work as I surrender to Your will and Your purpose. In Jesus's name I pray. Amen.

# Afterword

Thank you for taking this journey through the ABCs with me. I hope you have been blessed by our time together. I can so easily complicate what God intended to be simple. I think that's why He used the alphabet as an identity tool for me. I hope it helps you, too. I believe in His ability to change our identity one letter, one word, and one sentence at a time as we press into His Word and ask for new understanding. He has so much to say about who we really are. Do you know that He actually sees you as He created you? He sees you as you already are in Him; ask Him to open your eyes to His viewpoint.

As you move forward in your new identity, I encourage you to continue to seek truth from God's Word. Ask the Holy Spirit to lead you into all truth and every verse that describes you. Write it out. Take note of what you have in Jesus Christ. He died so you would walk in new life—your true identity.

Lord Jesus, I pray that every woman who has read this book will rise up into her true identity in Christ. Oh God, help us to surrender the old nature to You and walk in the newness of life. I pray for an awakening to the life You intended. If some readers don't yet know You as Savior, I pray they would repent of their sins and turn to You to receive the complete forgiveness you offer. If they don't know You as Lord over all of their life, I pray they would surrender all they are into Your tender care. Thank You, Jesus for making a way for us to come out of the desert and into the promised land. In Jesus's name I pray. Amen.

It's time to #beYOU.

God bless you,

*Kolleen*

209

## Connect with Kolleen

Website: **speakkolleen.com**

email: **kolleenlucariello@speakkolleen.com**

Facebook: **@speakkolleen** (Kolleen Lucariello, #theabcgirl)

# Notes

1   *Dictionary.com*, s.v. "Accepted," accessed January 17, 2020, http://dictionary.reference.com/browse/accepted/.

2   "G1344 - dikaioŌ - Strong's Greek Lexicon (KJV)," *Blue Letter Bible*, accessed 16 Jan, 2020, https://www.blueletterbible.org//lang/lexicon/lexicon.cfm?strongs=G1344&t=KJV Strong's/.

3   *Dictionary.com*, s.v. "Beauty," accessed January 17, 2020, https://www.dictionary.com/browse/beauty/.

4   "Dove Campaigns," Dove US, first accessed October, 2011, modified January, 2020, https://www.dove.com/us/en/stories/campaigns.html/.

5   *Merriam-Webster.com*, s.v. "Change," accessed January 17, 2020, https://www.merriam-webster.com/dictionary/change/.

6   *Merriam-Webster.com*, s.v. "Desire," accessed January 17, 2020, https://www.merriam-webster.com/dictionary/desire/.

7   "H3365 - yaqar - Strong's Hebrew Lexicon (KJV)," *Blue Letter Bible*, accessed 17 Jan, 2020, https://www.blueletterbible.org//lang/lexicon/lexicon.cfm?Strongs=H3365&t=KJV/.

8   *Merriam-Webster.com*, s.v. "Establish," accessed January 17, 2020, https://www.merriam-webster.com/dictionary/establish/.

9   "H6960 - qavah - Strong's Hebrew Lexicon (KJV)," *Blue Letter Bible*, accessed 17 Jan, 2020, https://www.blueletterbible.org//lang/lexicon/lexicon.cfm?Strongs=H6960&t=KJV/.

10  "H5553 - cela` - Strong's Hebrew Lexicon (KJV)," *Blue Letter Bible*, accessed 17 Jan, 2020, https://www.blueletterbible.org//lang/lexicon/lexicon.cfm?Strongs=H5553&t=KJV/.

11  *Merriam-Webster.com*, "Forgive," accessed January 17, 2020, https://www.merriam-webster.com/dictionary/forgive/.

12  Bryan Spicer, *For Richer or Poorer* (Universal City, CA: Universal Studios, 1997), film.

13  *Dictionary.com*, s.v. "Father," accessed January 17, 2020, https://www.dictionary.com/browse/father/.

14  *Merriam-Webster.com*, s.v. "Holy," accessed January 17, 2020, https://www.merriam-webster.com/dictionary/holy/.

15  *Dictionary.com*, s.v. "Image," accessed January 17, 2020, https://www.dictionary.com/browse/image/.

16   Neil S. Wilson, ed., *The Handbook of Bible Application* (Chicago: Tyndale House Publishers, Inc., 2000), pg. 314.

17   *Dictionary.com*, s.v. "Justified," accessed January 17, 2020, https://www.dictionary.com/browse/justified/.

18   *Dictionary.com*, s.v. "Absolve," accessed January 17, 2020, https://www.dictionary.com/browse/absolve/.

19   "G1344 - dikaioŌ - Strong's Greek Lexicon (KJV)," *Blue Letter Bible*, accessed January 17, 2020, https://www.blueletterbible. org//lang/lexicon/lexicon.cfm?Strongs=G1344&t=KJV/.

20   *Merriam-Webster.com*, s.v. "Know," accessed January 17, 2020, https://www.merriam-webster.com/dictionary/know/.

21   Don Stewart, "Who Were the Samaritans?," *Blue Letter Bible*, Last Modified April 24, 2007, https://www.blueletterbible.org/faq/ don_stewart/don_stewart_1319.cfm/.

22   *Dictionary.com*, s.v. "Love," accessed January 17, 2020, https:// www.dictionary.com/browse/love/.

23   *Dictionary.com*, s.v. "Mind," accessed January 17, 2020, https:// www.dictionary.com/browse/mind/.

24   Dr. Seuss, *Oh, the Thinks You Can Think!* (New York: Random House Books for Young Readers, 1975).

25   "G2507 - kathaireŌ - Strong's Greek Lexicon (KJV)," *Blue Letter Bible*, accessed January 17, 2020, https://www.blueletterbible. org//lang/lexicon/lexicon.cfm?Strongs=G2507&t=KJV/.

26   *Dictionary.com*, s.v. "Imagination," accessed January 17, 2020, https://www.dictionary.com/browse/imagination/.

27   "G3053 - logismos - Strong's Greek Lexicon (KJV)," *Blue Letter Bible*, accessed January 17, 2020, https://www.blueletterbible. org//lang/lexicon/lexicon.cfm?Strongs=G3053&t=KJV/.

28   *Dictionary.com*, s.v. "New," accessed January 17, 2020, https:// www.dictionary.com/browse/new/.

29   *Dictionary.com*, s.v. "Overcome," accessed January 17, 2020, https://www.dictionary.com/browse/overcome/.

30   "G3528 - nikaŌ - Strong's Greek Lexicon (KJV)," *Blue Letter Bible*, accessed January 17, 2020, https://www.blueletterbible.org// lang/lexicon/lexicon.cfm?Strongs=G3528&t=KJV/.

31   Smith Wigglesworth, "A Quote From Ever Increasing Faith," Goodreads, accessed January 17, 2020, https://www.goodreads.com/quotes/5085166-i-am-not-moved-by-what-i-see-i-am/.

32   *Dictionary.com*, s.v. "Purpose," accessed January 17, 2020, https://www.dictionary.com/browse/purpose/.

33   Rick Warren, *The Purpose Driven Life*, (Grand Rapids, MI: Zondervan, 2002), Pg. 17.

34   "Helen Keller Quotes," BrainyQuote, Xplore, accessed January 17, 2020, https://www.brainyquote.com/quotes/helen_keller_121539/.

35   *Dictionary.com*, s.v. "Qualified," accessed January 17, 2020, https://www.dictionary.com/browse/qualified/.

36   *Dictionary.com*, s.v. "Righteous," accessed January 17, 2020, https://www.dictionary.com/browse/righteous/.

37   *Dictionary.com*, s.v. "Righteousness," accessed January 17, 2020, https://www.dictionary.com/browse/righteousness/.

38   *Dictionary.com*, s.v. "Secure." Accessed January 17, 2020. https://www.dictionary.com/browse/secure/.

39   Arthur Schoenstadt, "Depression," eMedTV, originally accessed October 2011. Last updated January 29, 2017, http://depression.emedtv.com/depression/depression.html/.

40   *Dictionary.com*, s.v. "Treasure," accessed January 17, 2020, https://www.dictionary.com/browse/treasure/.

41   *Dictionary.com*, s.v. "Understand," accessed January 17, 2020, https://www.dictionary.com/browse/understand/.

42   "H2280 - chabash - Strong's Hebrew Lexicon (KJV)," *Blue Letter Bible*, accessed January 17, 2020, https://www.blueletterbible.org//lang/lexicon/lexicon.cfm?Strongs=H2280&t=KJV/.

43   *Merriam-Webster.com*, s.v. "Infection," accessed January 17, 2020, https://www.merriam-webster.com/dictionary/infection/.

44   "Texting: A Brilliant Way To Miscommunicate," *Higher Perspective*, November 22, 2019, https://www.higherperspectives.com/texting-brilliant-way-miscommunicate-2641417057.html/.

45   *Dictionary.com*, s.v. "Victorious," accessed January 17, 2020, https://www.dictionary.com/browse/victorious/.

46 *Dictionary.com*, s.v. "Wise," accessed January 17, 2020, https://www.dictionary.com/browse/wise/.

47 *Dictionary.com*, s.v. "Wisdom," accessed January 17, 2020, https://www.dictionary.com/browse/wisdom/.

48 "H3374 - yir'ah - Strong's Hebrew Lexicon (KJV)," *Blue Letter Bible*, accessed January 17, 2020, https://www.blueletterbible.org//lang/lexicon/lexicon.cfm?Strongs=H3374&t=KJV/.

49 *Dictionary.com*, s.v. "Exclude," accessed January 17, 2020, https://www.dictionary.com/browse/exclude/.

50 Stan and Jan Berenstain, *The Berenstain Bears and the Truth*, (NY: Random House Books for Young Readers, 1983).

51 *Dictionary.com*, s.v. "Yoke." Accessed January 17, 2020. https://www.dictionary.com/browse/yoke/.

52 Charles Finney, "Christ's Yoke Is Easy," (blog) *The Gospel Truth*, accessed January 17, 2020, https://www.gospeltruth.net/1861OE/610102_christs_yoke.htm.

53 *Dictionary.com*, s.v. "Zealous," accessed January 17, 2020, https://www.dictionary.com/browse/zealous/.

54 "G2206 - zēloō - Strong's Greek Lexicon (KJV)," *Blue Letter Bible*, accessed January 17, 2020, https://www.blueletterbible.org//lang/lexicon/lexicon.cfm?Strongs=G2206&t=KJV/.